Teaching Algebra
to Chickens

Pondering the Unanswerable
Questions of Life

By Don Peckham
Illustrated by Bill Keeling

To: Reggie

Don Peckham

933 - 8835

Teaching Algebra to Chickens
Pondering the Unanswerable Questions of Life
Copyright © 2011 by Don Peckham

Illustrated by Bill Keeling

Printing by Falcon Books

San Ramon, California
www.Falcon-Books.com

Paperback ISBN 978-0-615-41593-2
Hardbound ISBN 978-0-615-42092-9

PRINTED IN THE UNITED STATES OF AMERICA

Acknowledgments

My beautiful wife Lucy
Without her, I would not be the man I am today.

Bill Keeling
The illustrator of this book's original artwork and a lifelong friend.

Kim Pearson
The ghost writer who helped me put my thoughts into writing.

Susan Metters
Our literary talented daughter and the editor of this book.

Diana Morello
Computer whiz and typist extraordinaire.

Lucy and Don Peckham
September 6, 1986

Dedication

I dedicate this book to my number one inspiration and my wife of over 54 years, Mary Lou Peckham. Born Mary Luthella Logan, she was the mother of our three daughters, Janet, Nancy and Susan. She was also the proud grandmother to three blood-line grandchildren, three step-grandchildren and two adopted grandchildren.

Lucy's number one asset to me has always been her support and encouragement in most of my commercial endeavors that had promise, and discouragement of the ones she considered too harebrained to risk. When we jointly decided to plunge into a project she always gave every ounce of energy she had to reach beyond my own ability level, enabling us to succeed as a team. Many observers to some of our verbal sparring have wondered how we ever stayed married. Now that secret is out.

Sadly, Lucy passed away February 20, 2010. The last few years of her life she had major medical problems. It is evident now more than ever how heartwarmingly large her legions of friends and acquaintances really were.

Hats off to you, Lucy! We all loved you very, very much.

For those who don't know it, she was a major contributor to this book. She blessed this book even though she knew I'm probably the last person in history who has the qualifications to write anything literary. Some of her last words to me were, "Finish that book!" I'm trying, but it is very, very hard without her.

Thank you, Lucy. I really do love you almost as much as all those beautiful friends you accumulated over our very long lives.

Table of Contents

Chapter 1   Chickens or Sheep? · · · · · · · · · · · · · · · 9

Chapter 2   Is There a God? · · · · · · · · · · · · · · · 15

Chapter 3   Astronomy 101? · · · · · · · · · · · · · · · 21

Chapter 4   Who Are You? · · · · · · · · · · · · · · · · · 33

Chapter 5   Who Is Here With Us? · · · · · · · · · · · · 39

Chapter 6   How Does the Brain Work? · · · · · · · · · · 47

Chapter 7   What About Death? · · · · · · · · · · · · · · 51

Chapter 8   Which God? · · · · · · · · · · · · · · · · · · · 59

Chapter 9   Twinkle, Twinkle, Little Star? · · · · · · · · · 63

Chapter 10   What Will Replace Us? · · · · · · · · · · · · 69

Chapter 11   Can We Keep This Up? · · · · · · · · · · · · 75

Chapter 12   Who Owns What? · · · · · · · · · · · · · · · 81

Chapter 13   How Many Is Too Many? · · · · · · · · · · · 91

Chapter 14   Follow the Leader? · · · · · · · · · · · · · · · 97

Chapter 15   Why War? · · · · · · · · · · · · · · · · · · · 103

Chapter 16   What Is Justice? · · · · · · · · · · · · · · · 117

Chapter 17   Why Do We Work? · · · · · · · · · · · · · · 123

Chapter 18   Does Gender Matter? · · · · · · · · · · · · 131

Chapter 19   What If...? · · · · · · · · · · · · · · · · · · · 139

Chapter 20   Humpty Dumpty Earth? · · · · · · · · · · 145

Chapter One

Chickens or Sheep?

I always thought my cousin Allan Gardner was brighter than me. He was the intellectual in the family, at one time a candidate for Mensa. I liked to talk to him because he thought about things that I thought about too. The funny thing was he didn't have any more answers than I did.

One of the greatest conversations I had with Allan was in 1999, just a year before he died. He and his wife Miriam came to visit us in our home on the outskirts of San Francisco. Allan and Miriam lived in Georgia then, but our family has long roots in California. Allan grew up here, just as I did.

We went to the Presidio in San Francisco because that's where our grandfather Peckham is buried. Allan wanted to see the grave and neither of us had ever been there. Not so surprising for me, but Allan had been much closer to our grandfather than I had been.

My father and my grandfather had a falling out way before I was born, so I only met my grandfather a few times. The only thing I really knew about him was that he fought in the Spanish-American War in 1898, and the only reason I knew that was because somehow my dad ended up with his Army binoculars.

They weigh about 10 times what binoculars do now. I used to play with them when I was a kid and I still have them.

But Allan's mother, my father's sister, stayed on good terms with her father. So unlike me, Allan had lots of happy memories of our grandfather. Maybe it's easier between fathers and daughters than fathers and sons. I have three daughters and no sons, so I don't know. It's one of the things I think about, though.

Allan and I stood above our grandfather's grave, looking down at his headstone, not really talking much. It was a cool summer day, as summer days usually are in San Francisco. Our wives were off somewhere else, I don't know where — reading total strangers' headstones, I guess.

Standing there with Allan, both of us in our 70s and thinking about someone we had known who had fought in a war over a hundred years before — it makes you think. What's life all about? Why do we live and why do we die? Where did we come from and where do we go?

Because Allan and I used to talk about these things when we were kids, I said what I was thinking: "What's the point, and where is Grandpa now?"

Allan was quiet for a bit and then he said, "Explaining Creation to humans is like teaching algebra to a sheep."

I looked at him, and always wanting to have the last word, I said, "No, I think it's like teaching algebra to chickens."

We were laughing when our wives showed up a minute later. We walked back to the car and went home. That was the last time I saw Allan.

That conversation stayed with me though. Allan always had a way with words. He could say things and they stuck. Teaching algebra to chickens stuck with me. It kind of says it all.

I was never the intellectual that Allan was. He got a degree in engineering from the University of Wisconsin and I barely made it through two years of junior college. But later, after the war when we were men and not boys, I found success as a fly-by-the-seat-of-your-pants entrepreneur. I may not have been an intellectual, but I discovered I had plenty of business smarts and loads of ambition. Allan, on the other hand, used his verbal skills to build a career in sales.

Allan played with those philosophical questions and had an impressive command of language. I had to work to keep up with him when he really started talking. He was kind of like columnist George Will. If I were to get into a conversation with George Will I'd have to go back to college to enlarge my vocabulary. Otherwise I couldn't handle him.

But that doesn't mean I don't think about philosophical or scientific things. I've always thought about them. When I was a kid I was fascinated with space travel, as a lot of people were back then. I used to wonder what invaders from outer space would think of us Earthlings. Imagine if you were a space alien flying around in a saucer over the earth and heard all our radio conversations, in all the different languages. We can't even talk to each other. The aliens might think this was a crazy place to live. And they'd be right — it is.

I'm not sure why anyone from another planet would want to come here anyway. We're so insignificant those space aliens wouldn't bother. And as for us invading them, before we find out how to get to another planet we'd better deal with the mess we're making of our own. I don't think the other planets would want us. At least not the way we are now. Really, we're pretty much a bunch of cocky idiots. We think we're so great, but maybe we've just been lucky.

It seems obvious to me that our species is so limited and so small, compared to the immensity and variety of the universe, that we are foolish to pretend that we're somehow special. That's probably why I've never had much agreement with religion. I don't come from a religious family. My parents never talked about it much. Whenever I've come into contact with religious people, it seems to me that they are trying to take this huge thing

— God, the force that runs the universe, or whatever you want to call it — and put it into simplistic terms. They try to make God small like us, with a gender and a personality, who makes rules and laws and many pronouncements.

Religions try to find out the answers to those really big questions like "Where did we come from?" and "What happens after death?" and "What's the meaning of life?" Then when they find out they can't answer those questions, they make up some answers. That's okay, but I wish they wouldn't pretend that their made-up answers are the ultimate truth at the exclusion of all others.

I'd like to know the answers to those questions too, but I'm comfortable with knowing that I never will. Those answers are too big for me. Not because I'm not an intellectual, but because I'm human. I'm the chicken who can't learn algebra, and so is every other human. It's a waste of time to think we can. I'd much rather stand in awe at the interplay and beauty of every intricate detail of existence.

But I still go on asking the questions. That's also because I'm human. We're full of curiosity. Asking questions and trying to find the elusive answers is fun. It's one way we amuse ourselves.

And it's not only the big questions like the meaning of life, but the smaller ones that sometimes seem nearly as difficult. Such as "Why do we have so many wars?" or "Do animals have consciousness?" or "What are the real differences between men and women, and do they matter?" or "How can we conserve the earth's resources?" And a lot more.

The difference between the big questions and the small ones is that we actually have a chance of answering the small ones. I think that's where we should concentrate our energies.

You know what happens when we start asking questions? We become more aware. When we are aware, we can change things that need changing. When we are unaware, we are dangerous — to ourselves and to our planet.

These questions have been accumulating in my mind for over 80 years. Although I'm in good health, I'm also an octogenarian and I know I'm nearing the end of my time here. I don't know what comes next, if anything. This book is my way of kicking myself in the pants to get those questions out there.

My cousin and fellow philosopher, Allan Gardner.
March 24, 1924 – January 24, 2000.

I'm writing a book about the questions we should all be asking. I offer up some personal opinions about possible answers to these questions, but I'm not claiming these answers are the right ones. I didn't do any formal research and I'm not offering any proof. The answers — and the questions — are yours to be accepted or rejected.

So come up with your own answers, or your own questions. Together let's open our awareness.

Chapter Two

Is There a God?

Let's start with the Big Stuff and get it out of the way. God. The biggest stuff of all.

When she was only eight years old, my granddaughter Katie summed up my thoughts about God in one sentence.

"Grandpa," she said, "if God created everything, then who created God?"

Exactly.

I don't agree with those atheists who claim to know there is no God. How can they know? The answer is: they can't.

And I also don't agree with those religious fundamentalists — from *any* religion — who claim to know what and who and where God is. How can they know? The answer is: they can't either.

None of us can "know" anything about God.

January 31, 2007, was my 80th birthday. I celebrated by talking about the Big Stuff with my youngest daughter. She spent many years seeking out answers about God and at one point you could say she was a religious person. Maybe she would have said spiritual. Over the years, though, her thoughts on religion and God have evolved to be more in line with my own. Like me she has come to believe God is the ultimate unanswerable question. She still has plenty of opinions of her own and even though she doesn't attend church anymore I think she still prays to God. We don't always agree, but we're still talking to each other. And even though I don't pray, I think about God. I think about it a lot, actually.

I like to think of G – O – D as an acronym for Gravity, Orbits and Dimensions. All the gravity in the universe, all the orbiting bodies, all the dimensions and planes of existence are part of God. All of it. God is so big that even the terms you use to define God are themselves too big to define. If you assume God created everything, you have to realize "everything" is beyond comprehension. As an example, a newborn is born with over a trillion neurons in its brain. A baby is born with the mathematical mix and ability to function as a totally complete being, human or otherwise.

Just because God is so big — too big to really know what God is — doesn't mean there isn't one. Everything is so absolutely orderly and predictable it seems clear to me there must be a master designer.

It all comes down to this: you can't make something from nothing. Even the atheists will agree that the universe is definitely something. And that something had to come from somewhere. If you accept the Big Bang theory as true, as I consider possible, that infinitely dense mass of material that caused the original event had to come from something else. The shorthand for that something else is God.

Atheists believe that all of this something happened by itself. There is no creator and there never was. The order of the universe is just random. It just happened.

I don't understand how anyone can truly believe that. I think atheists just don't get it. Even if the atheists are scientists, you simply cannot make anything from nothing. Everything had to be made from something.

SORRY KATIE, I DON'T KNOW WHO MADE
GOD. GO ASK YOUR MOTHER!

I have a lot of respect for scientists because they look to science to answer the Big Stuff. Questions such as "Who created the universe? Where did it come from?" Good for them, I hope they keep looking. But so far all they've found are more questions. Eventually every one of those questions comes down to: you can't create something out of nothing. You need material to work with. Then the question becomes, "Where did that material come from?"

That's why I believe in God. I believe something had to create the universe and us within the universe. Otherwise, why is everything so orderly, so beautifully integrated? It can't just be an accident. Logic suggests there should be complete nothingness everywhere.

When my mother was in her 90s, she became philosophical. Maybe she finally had time to really think about things at last. "How is it," she wondered, "that if you plant an acorn, you always get an oak tree, regardless of the soil it's planted in? How can a caterpillar turn into a butterfly?" She wasn't asking for answers. She knew there were none. She was just marveling at the beauty and intricacy of all the forms of life.

I'm a practical man. I like to know how things work. And I'm practical enough to recognize my limitations. I believe there is a God, a creative force of some kind, an intelligent designer if you will, but I know it is way beyond my puny human comprehension. I don't need to try to define something that defies definition.

But if you were to try to define God or create a job description for God, I think it would look something like this:

- Exist forever — in the past, in the present, in the future, in infinite time.
- Exist simultaneously in every place in the universe, an infinite universe without edges or borders.
- Create everything from nothing.
- Have the time and energy to do the above, and then play a round of golf.

I differ with religious people in that I believe all the answers are not found in a book. I don't think religious people go far enough. They may label me an atheist, agnostic, or even infidel, but I do believe in God. With over 2000 religions in the human experience, there isn't a single one that answers my questions to my satisfaction. Some religious people are threatened by people like me. They don't like the mind-boggling questions without answers. It's so much easier, and feels so much safer, to let their religion give them some answers. They turn to their particular printed matter to tell them what it all means. But all the religious teachings on Earth come from human minds. Some will say their teachings are "inspired" by God, but to that I say, "Prove it!" They don't come from God. Does God write books? Come on.

Religions try to put God in simplistic terms and then they even go to war over their individual teachings. People are willing to die and kill over specific teachings that may or may not contain some truth. That's just crazy.

Anybody who claims they have an answer to the Big Stuff questions is either lying or deluded. We need to have respect for those things that have no answers.

Human beings are so arrogant. It's arrogant to make up something that looks like us, thinks like us and has concerns like us, then call it God, the Creator of all things. But if God was like us — had a form and a voice, made judgments and prohibitions, and rewarded and punished his creations — this is how I think an audience with God might go:

God: Cocky Human, I have summoned you to appear before me to discuss this experiment of my creation of mankind. I have been watching. It is showing alarming out-of-control characteristics.

Cocky Human: Thank you, Mr. God. I am honored to be in your lofty presence.

God: Just call me God, please. Gender titles don't work around here, Cocky. Let's cut to the chase. I created your planet with particular care about 4.5 billion of your years ago. I was precise with every detail, because I wanted to stock it with an environment ideally suited for life of all kinds to flourish. Everything was going along just fine until your particular species began showing signs of going out of irreversible control. You started attacking not only each other, but all other forms of life and the earth itself.

Cocky Human: But…

God: Be quiet. I gave your species a conscience, please use it! No more clubbing baby harp seals, no more boiling crabs alive, no more killing docile animals for amusement. You are only a peripheral part of my original plan. If you and the rest of your crowd don't realign your activities to appreciate and nurture the environment I created, I just may have to start over. Somewhere else...

Cocky Human: But...

God: Silence! Organized religion is another problem. Before we write off all religions, though, I hasten to encourage the peaceful teachings within every faith as a very positive force for good. But the destructive side of religion — the extremists, the violence, the hypocrisy — must be curbed. Now go back and use that meager IQ I gave you to work on saving what's left after the carnage you have done to my paradise. Now leave my presence before I lose my temper!

My granddaughter Katie at age 8.

Chapter Three

Astronomy 101?

Let's tackle a couple of other questions about the Big Stuff. What makes up our universe? How big is it? How many stars and planets does it contain? Do any of them, besides Earth, contain intelligent life? How can we find out?

More unanswerable questions, but we need to ask them.

We've come a long way from Galileo, who shocked the establishment when he suggested that the earth was not the center of everything. Now everyone accepts this. Earth is just one spot in the universe among billions of other spots, an average planet circling an average star in an outer arm of an average galaxy.

But if we all know this, why are we still so arrogant? I don't think most of us really realize how tiny a spot we occupy in the vastness of space. It's impossible for us to grasp the enormity of the universe, just as we're incapable of truly understanding God.

A few years ago a friend sent me an email that showed a graphic representation of the various sizes of planets and stars in our galaxy. It contained five separate pictures. The first showed the five smaller planets in our solar system — Earth, Venus, Mars, Mercury and Pluto (this was when Pluto was still considered a planet). Of these five, Earth is the largest, with Venus a close second. Mars is about half the size of Venus and then Mercury and Pluto are the smallest. We're the biggest — so do we win?

Hardly. The second picture shows all nine planets in the solar system. Suddenly Earth doesn't look so big. It's about a 10th of the size of Uranus and Neptune, and maybe a 50th of the size of Saturn. You could fit about a hundred Earths into Jupiter. Jupiter seems enormous.

Until you see the third picture, which is of the planets and our sun. The sun is a big orange ball and you could fit a couple hundred Jupiters into it, it's so large. Earth is a dot.

The fourth picture is a comparison of four different stars in our galaxy — the sun, Sirius, Pollux and Arcturus. Sirius is about 50 times the size of the sun, Pollux is about 50 times the size of Sirius and Arcturus must be a couple hundred times the size of Pollux. The sun looks pretty puny here.

It looks even punier on the last picture, which compares the sizes of eight stars in our galaxy, including the largest two — Betelgeuse and Antares. If you print this picture out on a piece of standard notebook paper, Antares and Betelgeuse take up two-thirds of the page at least. Antares is approximately 700 times the size of the sun. The printed picture of Antares and the sun would show Antares' diameter to be 10 centimeters and the sun just 1 pixel, smaller than the period at the end of this sentence. It makes you wonder how we are able to maintain our arrogance, but we do.

In addition, all these planets and stars are in our own galaxy, the Milky Way. A galaxy consists of stars, gas and dust, black holes and dark matter, (to understand what that is takes a more educated mind than mine), all bound together by gravity. The Milky Way is estimated to contain between 200 billion and 400 billion stars and is about 100 thousand light years in diameter.

Wait, there's more. It's estimated that there are 100 billion galaxies in the observable universe. (Observable by us — and you know our vision is pretty limited.) There is a googol more galaxies out there. And what is a googol? No, it's not an internet search engine. That's spelled "Google." The googol I'm talking about is a huge number used to describe the unimaginably vast. It's a 1 followed by 100 zeroes. It's said to be greater than the number of atoms in the visible universe (again, visible by us). The number of possible chess games is more than a googol. A black hole is thought to evaporate over eons of time, and a supermassive black hole would take about a googol of years to evaporate. You get the idea. A googol is a very, very large number. In practical Earth terms, a googol is a pretty useless number. But that's how many planets and stars and galaxies are out there with us: a googol of heavenly bodies.

Plus this doesn't count the space between the stars and galaxies, filled with more gas and dust, black holes, dark matter and things that have no names yet.

Finally, the universe has no borders. It has no frontier, no edges, nothing to fall off or fall through. It doesn't seem to stop. It just goes on and on and on — forever, in all directions.

It's going on at high speed, too. We can't feel it, but Planet Earth is orbiting the sun at 66,000 mph and at the same time our whole solar system is racing around the North Star at about 150,000 mph. The Milky Way, along with all the other googol of galaxies, is also zooming at incredible speeds around a center mass.

You'd think with all these stars and planets whizzing through space, there would be some we could visit, wouldn't you? But that's not the case. It's a long, long way from us to them. The closest celestial body is our moon, which is one and a half light seconds away. We're eleven light minutes away from our sun, and four light years away from Alpha Centauri, the nearest star that astronomers think may harbor something that could support our kind of life. Considering it's not even possible to travel at light speed — or anywhere remotely near it — it would take far longer than a lifetime to get there. It would literally take generations.

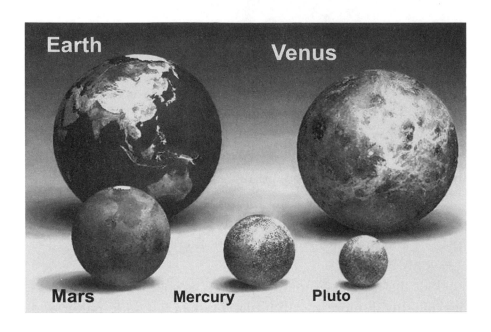

Models created by Gordon Speer

We were so awed by ourselves when we made it to the moon, only one and a half light seconds away. Well, it was awesome. I was as impressed as anyone else. But let's not let it go to our heads. One and a half light seconds is a long way from four light years.

So the universe is big, right? So big that our puny human minds have trouble comprehending it, even minds like Stephen Hawking's, however brilliant his mind is. And some scientists think that our universe with its googols of stars and matter may not be the only universe. Maybe there are parallel universes. Maybe if we could find a way to go through a black hole and warp the fabric of space-time, we would create new universes. Maybe the universe is part of a repeating cycle of Big Bang creation, leading to Big Bang destruction, leading again to Big Bang creation — no beginning and no end.

It boggles the mind, doesn't it?

It seemed a lot easier when I was a kid, thinking about space travel and extraterrestrials. I took it for granted that there were other beings out there and I didn't see any reason why we wouldn't someday meet up with them. I followed the comic book action figures of Buck Rogers and Flash Gordon and dreamed about traveling in outer space. Sometimes my friends and I would scan the sky for flying saucers. That was kid stuff, yet serious underneath.

I remember my mechanical drawing teacher in junior high. It was around 1942. One day he was explaining something and remarked, "You know that rocket ship Buck Rogers runs around in? They can actually do that." He went up to the blackboard and drew the chamber for ignition.

"It's not very efficient," he said. "It can only be thrust against the front wall and exhaust everything out the back. Around the belt line of the barrel everything cancels each other, so it wouldn't go very far in space."

But I was thinking, "That might work."

The teacher said, "It needs to have an independent fuel system. In the atmosphere, we need to have oxygen for most existing systems."

Regardless of my mechanical drawing teacher's rocket ship drawing and the feasibility present in the aerodynamics of flying saucers, as I learned more about astronomy and the distance between celestial bodies I came to realize that space travel is completely impractical. It's unlikely we'll ever visit another inhabited planet and they probably won't visit us either. There are just too many logistical requirements to get there. You'd have to take your whole environment with you. You'd need to take air to breathe and food to eat. It's not a job for United Van Lines.

But given the number (remember that googol) of stars and planets out there, of course there is probably other intelligent life somewhere. Maybe even relatively close, like orbiting Alpha Centauri. And I bet they're looking for others like themselves too. Maybe one day we'll discover each other.

I doubt it can be accomplished physically, though. At least not with our current technology. The distances and the time it would

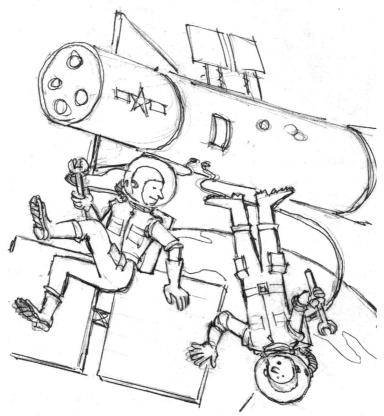

I JUST DON'T KNOW WHICH SIDE IS UP
ANYMORE.

take to travel them are just too vast. It'll probably be through some kind of mind transference, something like ESP or energy connections through the brain. Perhaps an intelligent creature on some far away planet will discover how to harness the power of the mind and they'll get in touch with us. Or we'll discover how to do it in the distant future. I wish I could be here to see it.

But maybe my children or grandchildren might see something started in the way of discovering inhabited planets. Many astronomers believe that the star Alpha Centauri has a good chance of having inhabitable planets. In the not too distant future, assuming we develop the technology to launch interstellar robotic probes, we might just send those probes on a mission to determine possible inhabitability. Of course, those voyages will still take several centuries, even if we develop spacecraft that are fast enough to do it at all.

Still, maybe my granddaughter Katie will witness the launch. Maybe her great-grandchildren will be there when the probe sends back word. Maybe, maybe! What a great word.

I'm actually not much of a reader; it's too passive for me. I like to look at things and figure out how they work, especially stuff I can get my hands on. I'm kind of a tinkerer. But I make exceptions for Stephen Hawking and Carl Sagan. I've read their books, even though I don't always understand them. They are big thinkers about big things, but they're practical men too. They want to know how things work so they can make things better, or fix what's broken.

That's why all this talk about space is important, especially right now. Even though we can't actually get our minds around the vastness of the universe and we don't understand all the elements that make it up — nor are we likely to ever understand all those elements — we can't just give up trying. We must keep on asking those big questions and trying to find some tangible answers.

Because sometime in the future — maybe the near future, or maybe a couple billion years from now — we are going to have to look for a new place to live if our species is going to survive. Let's face it — chances are we will have destroyed our planet by our own greed, carelessness, or violence. Either that or the sun will eventually die, as all things do, and take the earth with it. We don't have the technology now to get there, but we'd better start working on it.

Here is a list of requirements for a replacement planet:

- The planet needs to be reachable from our solar system, such as Alpha Centauri, over four light years away.

- It will need a solar system sufficiently organized to have the rescue planet in a circular orbit at about 90 million miles from its sun.

- The size of this planet should be similar to Earth with gravity near 1 G and a temperature range similar to Earth.

- It would also need water in abundance to foster the plant life required to generate an atmosphere that all land life requires, and marine life extracts directly from that water.

- The food sources must be compatible for our own needs.

Another important thing to consider is how to protect ourselves from alien diseases. Will we have to wear space suits? Create an elaborate biosphere? Maybe we can all just walk around in human-sized hamster balls. That might work.

Right now we're getting a good look at Mars. Maybe it had life on it at one point. I think they found evidence of water. Maybe it could support life again, who knows? Then we'd all be Martians!

Of course, living on Mars won't help us when the sun goes supernova, since we share the same sun. There are some scientists who believe that when the sun starts spinning into a supernova, we can tweak gravity a bit and change our orbit and maybe buy ourselves a few extra million years before we bite it.

When you start thinking about these things, Alpha Centauri starts looking pretty ideal. We better get to work. Fix the planet we're on right now while looking for a new one. We don't have much time.

Chapter Four

Who Are You?

It's a marvel to me that every single one of us is unique. No one else is just like you. Wouldn't it have been easier for God, that unknowable force, to make one template and then keep turning out little replicas? But that's not how it was done.

It would be easier on us too. Then maybe we wouldn't spend so much time trying to figure out just who we are. Am I my mind — my brain and my intelligence? Or am I my body — my legs and arms and heart? Or am I my feelings — my love, hate, envy or sadness? Or am I my soul — whatever that is?

Good questions. But again there are no answers.

Life gets switched on at conception and switched off at death. Each of us are conceived in a nanosecond, when we go from virtual nothingness to life. Both birth and death are random, at the mercy of infinite numbers — when yours is up, it's up. If all the bodies of water on earth were filled with alphabet soup and each letter was assigned one to an individual, you'd have only one in a googol's chance of being who you are. But look in a mirror — voilà! There you are.

Humans need to take a more realistic look at our individual gender assignments that began when our parents conceived each of us. Now males and females need to recognize there are

THE TRUE MEANING OF LIFE IS, IT'S A THREE RING CIRCUS.

very real differences beyond just instinctual attraction to each other. Clinically speaking, every single mammal that ever lived arrived at the birth moment after the required gestation period in its mother. The male role in conception is physically accomplished in a few moments with less than two pounds of male equipment. The female takes on the physical role of incubating the fetus until birth. She then nurses if she so chooses. A major percentage of her total body weight is devoted to the miracle of life. Pound for pound, females are stronger and live longer than males. The point of all this obviously is to keep in mind that this interplay requires mutual understanding and respect. So why is it that women have been held down in society? They have been humiliated over the centuries in horrible ways. Even in our own country, women weren't allowed to vote until the 1920s. Just think, none of us would be here without the role of women.

Half of us are female and half are male. If it's all so random, how is it so perfectly balanced? I wound up with three daughters and someone else may have three sons. I have three biological granddaughters and someone else has grandsons. I don't know what I have to do with any of this. Nothing, I think.

Why am I living now instead of a thousand years ago? Or a hundred, or a million years from now? I don't know. Do you?

We're different from other Earth creatures because we ask questions like this. We are what we call "intelligent" beings, which means we think more and better than other species. (At least that's what we tell ourselves.) We know now that some animals think nearly as well as we do, like dolphins and chimpanzees and dogs. We don't know much about how mosquitoes think, or squid, or maple trees, or carrots — although we are pretty sure they don't think. But that's what we thought about dolphins and chimpanzees and dogs, up until the last half century or so. The bottom line is that we exist in isolation from other forms of Earth life. We can't communicate with them. So why do we think we are so intelligent? And if we're so smart, why aren't we taking better care of our habitat?

I wasn't that close to my father. For one thing, he and my mother got divorced when I was 14 and after that I rarely saw him. Plus he was sort of abrasive — while he liked to think, he also liked to argue. But he still had influence on me. He's the one who got me started asking questions.

That's the way I think we humans should use our intelligence. When we're children, we should use our intelligence to learn. Then when we get to adulthood we should be using it to produce and add something valuable to the world. And then when we're old we should use it to mentor the upcoming producers, to pass along our knowledge. In that way we build on each generation.

There are many photographs of me as a youngster. The one of me that captures my love of life is me in a baby carriage with eyes as big as headlights. It's a good metaphor for my whole life. I've always been in awe of the wonders I saw around me.

Even at 7½ months I was in awe of the world. *September, 1927.*

I don't think our brains are the most important thing about us. I think what's really important is that we are self-aware. As far as we know, self-awareness isn't shared by many other creatures. But maybe it is. How would we know? That's another question to explore.

I'm also interested in when awareness begins. Does it begin at birth, the moment we take our first breath and feel the cool air hit our skin? Or does it begin before that, when we're in the womb? Or maybe at the moment of conception, when the sperm meets the egg? Just because we can't remember when we were a fetus doesn't mean we didn't have thoughts and feelings at that stage. After all, we can't remember our babyhood either. But I don't think anyone would argue that babies don't have feelings and thoughts. In fact, babies are all feelings and thoughts.

These are controversial topics. The subject of abortion gets everyone all riled up on both sides. I believe that women have the right to choose what to do with their own bodies, but I don't think we've answered the question about when life begins — at least not to my satisfaction. We should take politics and religion out of this subject and make it a medical responsibility. I strongly believe that!

I don't know the right answer to this controversial question. But I also don't think it's helpful to take such a strong position on the subject that we can't listen to each other's opinions. If we don't try to learn with open minds we'll never discover the answer and we'll end up fighting and hating each other forever. What's the good in that?

So when does life begin — any life, aware or not? It's a question that's not so easy to answer. I remember reading about some archaeologists who found a vessel in an Egyptian tomb and in the vessel were some seeds. The seeds were rye seeds, of a low-grade variety that had been extinct for thousands of years. Yet when they planted those seeds, they sprouted and grew.

Life was there all those years, just waiting for the right conditions. If this is true of a rye seed, wouldn't it be true of a human being? Now we're freezing human sperm and eggs. If frozen sperm and frozen eggs from today were put together a thousand years from now and a new human was born, would that human be from today or from tomorrow? Just think if your father and mother had been dead for a thousand years by the time you were born. Would you be an anachronism in your own time? Maybe it wouldn't be so easy to know which time was your time.

We can now actually decide when we want to conceive a new life. We can clone new lives from old ones. We can crossbreed species of plants and animals to create new forms. Does this mean that we are gods?

I don't think so. We might be able to plant the seeds, or manipulate them, but we can't start from nothing and make new seeds. Thomas Edison once said, "Until man duplicates a blade of grass, nature can laugh at his so-called scientific knowledge." We can't make a blade of grass. I'm glad we can't, because until we can answer the question "what is life?" we shouldn't jump ahead of ourselves.

Chapter Five

Who Is Here With Us?

It was a shock for us to learn that we're not the center of the universe. It is difficult for human beings to accept that we're not even at the center of our own solar system. Many of us haven't accepted it yet. We act as if Earth was created with us in mind, a personal playground made just for humans. We seem to think that we are the end of a long chain, the ultimate aim of creation. But we need to acknowledge that this is not really true. There are other creatures here on Earth, most of them here much longer than us, who might have a different opinion. Maybe the ants think that Earth belongs to them. To them, humanity might just be a noisy, destructive newcomer who hasn't died off yet. Who's to say the ant isn't the one it's all about?

Maybe it's inevitable that each species thinks it's all about them. So if we're cocky right now, at least we're still learning. It was only about 500 years ago that people were saying, "The earth is flat. Don't go too far or you'll fall off." Five hundred years is nothing in terms of astronomical time, a mere split second. We've come a long way since then.

We are all related. No one species is better or more important than another, just different. Now they've found evidence there used to be water on Mars, so maybe even Mars had life at one time. That's where we all came from, according to evolutionary theory — we came from the water. Although I have to admit that I find this theory difficult to get my mind around. It takes some imagination to picture it. The bottom line for me is, we all arrived here on Earth — or Mars — in some way. I'm not sure we can figure it out ourselves.

But here we are all together. Humans, elephants, frogs and mosquitoes, plus a couple million other species. Yet after millions of years together, we still haven't figured out how to communicate with each other.

We humans think we are special because we have opposable thumbs that allowed us to develop tools (and weapons) and a larynx that allowed us to develop a complex spoken language. We thought we were so special that we didn't think we needed to communicate with the other inhabitants of the planet. Who cared what they thought? Mostly we just ate them, if we could kill them without being killed ourselves.

In fact, it's only in the last few years that humans have even tried to communicate much with the so-called lower animals. Now we can get a dog to sit up and roll over. But that's about as talented as we get in interspecies communications.

The lower animals are better at this than we are. You probably think you know your dog, but I would bet your dog knows you a whole lot better. We've taught chimps to speak American Sign Language, but as far as I know not one human has learned to speak chimpanzee.

My sister's father-in-law went with Admiral Byrd's expedition to Antarctica in 1939. He was a scientist studying dolphins and he thought that dolphins had their own language and were talking to each other. He felt they were smart enough. When I was in the Navy, I was a sonar man. I listened to whales and dolphins sing in their squeaky, high-pitched voices. At the time, in 1945, it didn't occur to me that they were talking to each other. But now there are scientists who say they have proven what my sister's

father-in-law believed. Those dolphins and whales are communicating with each other in a highly sophisticated way.

Now this doesn't mean that they have developed grammar and pronunciation rules, or can refer to hundreds of different fish by distinct names, or can conduct philosophic discussions about the nature of love. At least not as far as we know. But of course, one thing that we have proven beyond a doubt is that "as far as we know" often doesn't go far enough.

Many of the other forms of life have far better physical assets than humans do. Hawks can spot a mouse running on the ground from 2,000 feet above. Cheetahs run fast enough to get arrested for speeding. Birds were flying when the dinosaurs were around but man couldn't figure out how to do it until the 20th century. A dog's sense of smell is nearly a thousand times more sensitive than ours. And so on.

DOLPHINS COMMUNICATE

I'M HEADING FOR SHORE,
I GOT A CRAMP IN MY LEFT
PECTORAL FIN.

YOU HEAR ABOUT HAZEL? IT'S SCANDALOUS.
SHE RAN OFF WITH A SPERM WHALE!

Ah, but we have those extra special brains! And it is true that our brains are amazing, no doubt about it. Yet the lower animals have brains too; all mammals, amphibians, reptiles, birds, fish and even insects. Think of ants and bees with their complex social structures that we still don't quite understand. Maybe even plants have brains; maybe even bacteria. These other creatures' brains are different from ours, but does that mean they are lesser? Maybe not.

It's clear that one big difference between the animal "them" and the human "us" is that animals don't seem to deliberately alter their environment the way we do. They don't go around recklessly tearing down old things and building new things just because they can. Although a big herd of elephants can do a lot of damage to the vegetation as they migrate, they don't poison the land itself, so nothing will grow again. Like we often do.

The debate about animal intelligence relative to humans will go on for a long time. We don't want to give up our claim to being the smartest creature on the planet. Nevertheless, recently our conception of animal brains has changed drastically. We now admit that they have feelings. Not only do they feel physical pain, they experience emotions. Elephants grieve. Cows mourn. Cats get embarrassed. Chimpanzees play tricks and then laugh at their own jokes. The fact that animals — and not only mammals — experience what we would call emotion has huge implications on how we interact with them and use them. Or eat them.

If animals — all animals, including insects and fish — think and feel, what does that say about us in terms of cruelty and brutality? Can we still think of hunting and fishing as a sport? As something we do for fun?

When I was about five or six years old, I went fishing with my father and some friends of his out on San Francisco Bay. One of the men caught a fish about six inches long. They hauled the fish in and dumped it on the bottom of the boat, right by my feet. It flopped around frantically, dying in front of my eyes. It had a hook in its mouth and kept gasping for the water that wasn't there. I couldn't take my eyes off it while I listened to all those grown men laughing at that poor fish.

If I close my eyes now I can still see that fish dying at my feet. I still feel guilty and ashamed and absolutely furious about what was done to that defenseless creature. That was the one and only time I went fishing.

The first time I went to Fisherman's Wharf in San Francisco, when I was a teenager, I saw crabs being boiled alive. They don't die immediately, you know. While they're being boiled they scream and try to scramble out of the pot, only to be pushed back down by the cook. Some people think that when we eat animals that have died in terror, we ingest that same energy. In some other cultures they even eat animals when they are still alive and wiggling.

Most cultures frown on cannibalism, but if animals are aware and conscious, with feelings and ways to communicate, then what's the difference between eating them and eating other humans? I don't have an answer to this problem of how to be a carnivorous animal like us and yet preserve a brotherly feeling toward other forms of life.

By now you're probably thinking I'm some kind of self-righteous vegetarian. I'm not. I eat fish and chicken and cows and pigs. I enjoy crab meat, even though I know they are killed in a barbaric act of stunning cruelty. How can I do this if I feel this way? The truth is I'm a hypocrite. I enjoy meat; I just don't want to be the one to kill it. It's easy to ignore the truth when you're at the store buying a steak in a nice little package. It doesn't look like a cow at all anymore, so I can turn a blind eye and enjoy my steak. I think it's easy for all of us to turn a blind eye, so we do.

I think we need to find another way to kill animals we eat, so crabs, for instance, don't boil alive in pain and horror. If we need to eat them, animals should be killed without brutality. They deserve at least as much dignity and painlessness as we give the criminals we execute. Although for much of human history, we have treated each other badly. We don't hang, draw and quarter any more. We need to apply these same standards to the animals we use for food.

The animals have a right to be here on the earth, same as us. They don't exist just to feed us or serve us. They exist for their own sake, to enjoy their lives. But for most of human history we haven't known that and now we're looking at an earth where wild animals are dying off — and we're going to miss them when they are gone. It's possible that we might not be able to survive without them.

I live in a middle class suburban tract development, in a nice house with nice landscaping and a bunch of neighbors with the same. There's a lot of shrubbery and well-tended gardens. One of the things we complain about is that the deer eat our rosebushes.

Some of my neighbors have cats, and they complain about the raccoons that come up through the storm drains and into the neighborhood where they kill their cats and go through the garbage. Possums come out at night and you'll see their corpses on the highways in the mornings. Last spring a mama bird built her nest in the tree right outside our bedroom window. Last fall four wild turkeys walked down the middle of our street one morning, gobbling up a storm.

They're out there existing, the wild right in our front yards, and most of what we do is complain about them. Why? They're as much a part of nature as we are. Life is everywhere. When I see a worm on the ground after a rain, I step around, because he has a life too. I had a black widow spider make her nest in my sprinkler system control box. She wasn't hurting anybody so I let her be. I say let them all be.

I didn't always think this way. Forty years ago I had a war with the gophers, moles and raccoons that came into our yard and dug holes all over. While I trapped the raccoons in a humane trap and let them loose out in the hills, I have to admit I put poison on a carrot and put the carrots in the gopher holes. Now I regret doing that. I wouldn't do it today. I learned better and I hope the gophers forgive me.

Chapter Six

How Does the Brain Work?

Anyone who has been married for more than a few years knows that we can learn to read minds. I remember there would be times when my wife and I would not talk about a particular subject for weeks or months. Then one day I'd come in the door and open my mouth to say something about this subject, but she'd beat me to it by saying the same thing I was going to.

Or one night you'll have a dream about a friend you haven't seen or thought of in years and the next day the telephone rings and it's him. Or the telephone rings and you immediately know who is on the line, before you pick it up. This kind of simple mind reading happens to everyone at one time or another. We all know it exists.

It's not something I can explain, though. I don't know how it works, which kind of bothers me because I always like to know how things work.

I'm not alone. Most human beings want explanations for why and how things happen. We are uncomfortable when we're confronted by people who claim to have a sixth sense like precognition, which is foretelling the future; or telepathy, sensing thoughts or feelings without use of our five senses; or clairvoyance, which is knowledge about people or things without the use of those five senses. Or even people who claim to be mediums and can talk to the dead, or sense the presence of ghosts.

Many of us want to write off these so-called abilities. I think this skepticism is healthy. And yet, some of this stuff has happened to me. So I'm left with another question without an answer. It's another algebra class for chickens.

I don't buy the supernatural explanation. If many of us observe it, over and over again, then it must be a natural phenomenon. Our level of understanding is just not there yet. We aren't done evolving and in a couple of thousand or million years, maybe people (or whatever comes after people) won't have a spoken language at all; maybe they'll communicate by just thinking at each other. I'd like to be around to experience that.

It's not just humans who have this sixth (or seventh or eighth) sense. Probably all animals have them, but we know for sure that dogs and horses do. They know when earthquakes or other natural disasters are coming, long before the event happens. They can sense illness, or even ill-temper, in the humans they are close to. They often know when someone they love has died — even if the person is a long way away. Or they know when a person is going to die — dogs have been known to howl before a loved one's death. They know when their people are coming home, before they get there. Our dog Penny always knew when I was going to take her for a walk — and she wasn't tipped off by cues like putting on walking shoes. Penny started reacting when I decided — in my mind alone — that it was time for a walk.

What all this shows is that we don't understand time and space as we think we do. We're definitely missing something. I would like to see more hard scientific research done on the sixth sense, and have it be taken seriously by the scientific community.

Every form of life that reacts to danger, pain, temperature, etc., has a brain unique to survive in their own environment. But in the human experience we do have one huge advantage over other life forms. Our ability to collect our thoughts through speech, and to build on past and present experiences, enables us to create a collective intelligence. Individually we may not have a much higher IQ than some animals, but collectively we can multiply our mentality to the point that we humans alone control a major influence over changes to our environment. That may be our Achilles' heel.

In other areas of brain function we are no match for the sheer athletic power, reflexes, visual acuity, etc., of animals. Bears have torn trunks off of automobiles to reach food they could smell. Whales have been known to inflict major damage to small ships. The reaction time of a mongoose against a cobra is lightning fast.

In most physical functions nothing but thought creates instant brain commands. You feel something hot, you react immediately. No buttons or pedals to push, no handles to pull. Your reflex is automatic. You itch somewhere and without conscious thought your brain dispatches the necessary digit to scratch it.

You learn a new skill such as driving a car. At first you pay close attention when your instructor tells you to "start your engine." You put the key into the ignition. Then turn the key to start the engine. "Fasten your seat belt. Now put your right foot on the brake as you put the transmission in reverse." But the more you practice this and the more skillful you become, the more you do all the correct physical functions automatically and then subconsciously.

Now the lower animals — bugs, birds, snakes, marine life, etc. — have brains too. Their reaction time varies from species to species. We get frustrated trying to swat flies. That fly is only a few days old, yet manages to evade us until we use a swatter or an electronic zapper. Now in this scenario the IQ differential is not obvious. That fly's brain keeps him on the move every time you come near.

Another example: on January 15, 2009, an airliner over New York City encountered a flock of very large birds. We all marveled at the unbelievable and heroic outcome of that event. Due to the miraculous actions of pilot "Sully" Sullenberger and his heroic crew, they prevented the loss of human life when they bravely landed the aircraft safely on the Hudson River.

The birds, however, didn't fare so well. They lost several of their number by flying into the path of the jet engines that delivered a coup de grâce instantly and as effectively as a wood chipper. This brings forth the question: how do birds of any size communicate with each other, in order to form large formations led by what appears to be a single leader?

In-flight V formations are beautiful to watch, but how do they execute instant changes of direction en mass? These sweeping changes seem beautifully choreographed, apparently directed by the lead bird, but how the next move is communicated to the rest of the flock is a mystery. If we could only get inside those tiny brains we just may find an aviary solution that could control these peaceful birds to see them reach their destination without encountering human built wings. Then maybe future encounters can be reduced or ideally totally avoided. Radar on the human side works only to a point.

We know a newborn human has trillions of neurons at birth. How does the brain become a thinking, functioning organ so intricately complete that it controls every part of a living human as well as in all forms of mobile life? After all, each life began with just two cells. At birth the brain is connected to every part of the body. The automatic functions of the heart, lungs, digestive system, etc., are already launched and will function mainly without conscious attention throughout life.

Controlled mobility — such as walking, sitting, squinting or talking — and all physical movement are controlled by the brain, although we do these things mostly without consciously thinking about it as well. What sets us apart are our conscious thinking processes and deliberate choices. These alone make us the commander and chief of our own actions.

Chapter Seven

What About Death?

Nowadays I often wake up early in the morning thinking about death. I see that Reaper coming down the line and he's not that far off. I'm in good health and both my parents broke through the 90 year barrier before they expired, but 90 isn't even 10 years away from where I am now. Ten years goes by zip — just like that. Ten years is nothing.

The idea for this book started when my cousin Allan and I were standing over a grave wondering where the inhabitant was now that he was dead. Death is something we all think about at one time or another, even when we pretend not to. That's because it scares us. It's the ultimate unknown, isn't it?

Of course, many people — maybe most people — tell themselves pretty stories about what comes next. Heaven for the good guys and Hell for the bad — that's what the Christians say, anyway. And the Muslims and Jews too, I think. The Buddhists say we'll reach nirvana, where everything is perfect, but only after we've been reincarnated several times. The Hindus believe in reincarnation too. The nonreligious people wonder about the essense or energy that may survive after death. And of course there are those who see or talk to ghosts and believe that some poor souls wander the earth forever.

YOUR RECENTLY DECEASED EX-WIFE TOLD
ME TO TELL YOU TO GO STRAIGHT TO HELL.

OH GOD, NOT ANOTHER ONE!

Even those scientists who study near-death experiences, which seem to suggest something is happening after death, can't prove anything is. And the atheists say that there's nothing happening after death — when you're gone, you're gone, and that's it.

Really, these are all just guesses. We can't know for certain (at least not yet) what, if anything, happens to our soul or essence or energy after we die. We all have to sit tight and wait to find out.

Two famous people, Ernest Hemingway the author and Gary Cooper the movie star, were said to have an agreement with each other that the first deceased would try to communicate with the survivor. Another famous person, Harry Houdini, was said to have the same agreement with his mother. In both cases, there hasn't been any indication of success in fulfilling these agreements.

Most of us are not that good at waiting. We're impatient and we want to know right now. But we never will, just like chickens will never learn algebra. I think we should get used to it. That doesn't mean we should stop thinking about death, though. For one thing, it's impossible, especially when you get to be my age. I wonder about the possibilities too, as does everyone else. I just don't think I'm going to find out until it happens.

But there are plenty of things we do know about death and those bear thinking about also. For instance, we certainly know what happens to our bodies after we die. They rot and turn into fertilizer just like the dead leaves, bugs and apple peels that make up a compost pile. At least they would if we let them. But since decomposing bodies smell about as bad as anything on Earth, we have figured out other ways to deal with them. There are a lot of laws about how you can or cannot discard the dead. Some of these laws make sense, but some of them are just the government butting in where it doesn't belong.

The way we dispose of the dead varies with culture and time, but basically we either bury them in the earth or burn them. When I was younger the only exception was if someone died at sea, where neither of those options was open. Those bodies were consigned to the deep to nourish the fish. Of course, if today you died at sea you probably wouldn't be dumped overboard. Your body would be stored and shipped to your home so your family could carry out your last wishes and either burn or bury you. So the burn or bury option is one we should all consider. Not everyone agrees on which way is better.

Cemeteries are peaceful places, good for contemplating the nature of life and gaining perspective. The problem with burial is that it takes up too much land. Just think of all that good land dedicated to dead people, who probably don't appreciate it. When John Kennedy was president it was estimated that the existing living population represented 4% of all humans that ever lived. That means that 96% have been disposed of. If the planet is going to be around a few billion more years we have to stop burying people in the ground. Not to mention the money spent on burial is nonsense. Gorgeous caskets and chemically embalmed, made-up corpses end up disappearing into holes and no one ever sees them again. And the holes are lined with cement or other materials; not exactly environmentally friendly.

Now there are some "green" cemeteries where the burials are more natural. They wrap the dead body in a burlap sack or something like that, something biodegradable. Then they plant the body next to a tree or something green and growing, far enough down so animals can't dig it up. The body degrades and nourishes the earth. This sounds better to me, but it's not legal in every state. Death is regulated. I guess they're afraid that once you open that door, people will just plant Mom or Dad in the backyard. You just can't have stray skeletons turning up all over the place.

Then there's cremation. This doesn't take up so much acreage and it's not as expensive. But cremation is not always the best environmental option either. You end up with problems with emissions polluting the air. The fumes and the smoke from burning bodies aren't pleasant.

I remember when my cousin Gordon Fisk died. Gordon was my chief business mentor and one of those type A personalities who lived to work. He was only 61 when he died on a tennis court of a massive heart attack. He threw the ball up in the air to serve and was dead before the ball hit the ground. After he was cremated, about 10 of his friends and family loaded up my tool truck with a couple of bags of cement, a bronze plaque and some lumber. Then we drove to the cemetery in Rescue, California, where most of that part of the family is buried. We dug a hole and turned to the widow. She had a cardboard box with Gordon's ashes in it, but she hadn't opened the box yet so none of us knew what to expect.

She opened the box and pulled out a plastic baggie. We all just looked at it and the widow said, "That isn't Gordon, is it?" But it was. Someone suggested we just open the baggie and pour the contents on the ground. That didn't sound right, so we just sat around trying to figure out what to do. Finally we put the baggie back in the cardboard box and buried the box. We mixed the cement and placed the bronze plaque. I hope what we did pleased Gordon, but who knows?

When I die, I want to go back to the earth. I'll be cremated, but I don't want to sit in an urn on somebody's mantle. I'd probably just be passed down from generation to generation until someday someone throws me out with the garbage or leaves me in an attic. I don't want to take up space in a cemetery either. I want to be sprinkled someplace where my ashes can do some good. I'd like to be sprinkled on a vineyard or a strawberry patch. Of course, this is illegal and my two daughters who are in law enforcement have made sure I know this. But my youngest daughter is more flexible, like me. She says that maybe she and a friend of ours will grab a six- pack some night and sneak out to a vineyard or strawberry patch with my ashes. They'll wear black clothes and sit around and tell jokes and share funny memories of me while I float on the wind and drift down onto the grapes or strawberries. That's how I'd like to come back — through the food chain. I'll be a part of some wine or breakfast fruit. What could be better than that? I'd like that, but of course I may not know anything about it.

Some people are interested in cryogenics and cryopreservation, the technology of preserving dead bodies by freezing them. The theory is that the dead could be revived later when new medical techniques can cure whatever killed that body in the first place. This raises some questions. What about aging? Our bodies aren't built to last forever. If you were frozen when you were old you probably wouldn't live much longer anyway. So what's the point in that? Unless scientists also developed a way to halt the aging process, cryogenics would really only be worthwhile for those who died when they were young. Otherwise you'd be revived and still be 90, have only a few years left to live and everyone you know would still be dead. Who wants to make a whole new set of friends when they're 90? Not to mention having to learn a whole new way of life since obviously society will have changed dramatically while you were dead. I sure wouldn't.

We humans are always trying to manipulate everything, even death. I think this raises more disturbing questions. What if this succeeds and no one ever died? How long would it take us to overrun the earth? How long would the food, the air, or the water last? Would we have to stop new births? Think of the stagnation of new ideas that would cause.

Here's what I think is the important truth about what comes next. Our descendants are important. They will build on what we have created, just as we have built upon our ancestors' achievements. I'm kind of interested in genealogy. We can trace a branch of my family, the Peckhams, back to before the Norman Conquest, about a thousand years. Peckhams have been in America since 1640 and in California since the 1840s. That's a lot of Peckhams. And every one of them contributed something, even if it isn't recorded. Who I am today, who my children and grand-children are, owe a lot to those who came before us.

So many of us don't share ourselves with our children. We're too busy making a living or trying to survive. It's kind of sad. After my cousin Allan died, his daughter called me to ask me questions about her dad. She said she never knew much about him. I was surprised because Allan was important to me and I remembered so much about the things he said and shared with me. I know that his life made a difference.

I would like to think this book about my thoughts and actions will become important to my descendants, that it will give them some sense of belonging. That's what really comes next after you die — sons and daughters and grandsons and granddaughters, hopefully building on what you did, improving it and passing it along. That's the real immortality.

HE STILL OWES ME
TWENTY BUCKS.

Chapter Eight

Which God?

Earlier I wrote about whether there was a God or not. I don't know the answer to that question, although I believe there must be something. I don't know what that something is. However, many people think they do know. The problem is that the something for one group of people is often different from the something for another group of people.

That's where religion comes in. Religions define the something and call it God, and people believe them because they want answers. But religions have all evolved out of human minds and the real reason for their existence is not to give people answers, but to organize and lead the people.

There are no answers to the questions, "Who is God?" and "What does God want?" No one knows. All the answers given by the various religions are either guesses or deliberately made-up stories.

Maybe it was the way I was brought up that makes me think this way. My parents weren't antireligious, they just didn't seem to care about it one way or the other. I was actually baptized in a little community church in a town of about 150 people, but my parents only had me baptized because that was what you did back then. It was more of a social rite than a religious one. I don't remember going to Sunday school or church very often as a kid. Sundays were a day of play for me.

I think that's true of a lot of people. They go to church because that's how they were brought up, not because they've researched all the world's religions and decided on the best one. Religious beliefs seem to be influenced more by culture and geography than by anything else. Why else would India be largely Hindu, the Middle East largely Muslim, China largely Buddhist and America largely Christian? I guess if there's really only one "right" religion then you'd better hope you were born in the "right" country.

When my kids were growing up I did the same as my parents. I didn't push religion, but they were free to attend church if they wanted to. All three of them went through a time when they were interested in religion and each of them chose to be baptized on their own. None of them are very religious now, but they all believe in God.

I've met a lot of religious people throughout my life. Often somebody would quote the Bible to me and be shocked when I didn't recognize their quotation. I've never read the Bible and in some circles that's not acceptable. But I refuse to lie about it and tell people I am a Bible-loving Christian just so they'll feel more comfortable.

I'm not against Christians, or Jews, or Buddhists, or any form of religious practitioners. I agree with the US Constitution that we're all free to practice any kind of worship we choose. I've met and liked many religious people. I work with a great guy who is a Mormon and he is one of my favorite people to work with. He is always upbeat and happy, cracking jokes all the time and he is also one of the most honest people I've ever met. What he says he'll do, he'll do — on time and perfectly. I wish all my working relationships were with people like him.

He is open about his religion and how important it is to him, but he never pushes it on me, or on anyone. And he doesn't get upset when I express my views either. It seems like that's how it should be.

The feature that irritates me most about religions is the way they seem to think it's important that everyone agree with them about who God is and what God wants. I hate simplistic explanations. When my mother was in her last years she hired a woman to come to her home to help take care of her. This woman was very religious and she preached her brand of religion day and night to my mother. And the feebler my mother became, the more she fell under the influence of her caregiver. Probably the woman thought she was saving my mother's soul, but when she tried to save my soul too, I tactfully told her to leave me alone.

One overly religious person trying to save an old woman's soul is a fairly benign example of religious fervor, of course. But the history of all religions is far from benign. There are over 2,000 religions in the world and every one of them thinks the rest are all wrong — and some of them are willing to kill the others to show how right they are. Catholics and Protestants, both Christians, blew each other up for centuries over their different interpretations of the words of one man. Six million Jews were murdered just for being Jews. Sunnis and Shiites, both Muslims, blow each other up today, again over their interpretations of the words of one man. And on and on — every religion is steeped in blood. Does this make sense to you? It sure doesn't to me.

It's simplistic to think that religious wars are only about differing beliefs. After all, most religions preach the values of peace and love. They all value honesty and sobriety, respect for elders and family, kindness and compassion. This part of religion should be encouraged.

But these shared values are not what religious wars are based on. Religious wars are really based on what all wars are based on — greed and lust for power. War might wear a cloak of religious fervor, but underneath the cloak is always money and power. Some king wanted more land, or some rich country wanted more oil, or some tyrant wanted everyone in the world to bow down to him and kiss his rear end. But he can't tell his soldiers that's what he wants, so instead he tells them that the other guy's God is a false God and the only true God is their own. Or if they want to go to Heaven they have to fight for their God and kill everyone who doesn't believe the "right" way. And if that doesn't work, the warmonger makes big promises like "God will reward you with the wealth of our enemy," or "Treasures await you in Heaven," or big threats like "Fight for our God or your family will suffer."

This has been happening for all of human history. Bad guys like Osama bin Laden didn't invent this way of motivating followers. The Christian Crusades of the 12th century were exactly the same at heart as Islamic terrorism is today. People are motivated by three basic things: 1) greed — "I want what the other guy has," 2) fear — "If I don't kill them they're going to kill me," and 3) love — "If I don't fight my children won't eat." A smart warmonger, such as Osama bin Laden, will use all these motivators to get people to carry out his perverted agenda. And since religion contains ways to use all these motivators, it is the perfect cloak for power lust.

We need to be aware of how religion is being used against humanity. This doesn't mean I think we should get rid of religion entirely. There's a lot of good to be found in religious philosophy — especially things like "love thy neighbor." But we must not allow ourselves to become so invested in our philosophy that we are willing to murder in its name. We need to be able to talk about our religions, honesty and openly, and express why they work for us. But if the other guy likes his God better than ours, we have to let him go his own way.

Chapter Nine

Twinkle, Twinkle, Little Star?

My father was a schoolteacher in love with words. He liked to play word games with my sister and me and these memories are among the best I have of him. He taught us two verses to "Twinkle, Twinkle, Little Star" — the first verse was the common version, and the second verse was what Dad called the "prodigy version." It went like this:

Common version:
>Twinkle, twinkle, little star
>How I wonder what you are
>Up above the world so high
>Like a diamond in the sky.

Prodigy version:
>Scintillate, scintillate, globular vivific
>Feign would I fathom thy nature pacific
>Poised aloft in the ether capacious
>Strongly resembling a gem carbonaceous.

I taught my own kids these verses too, as well as other word games and songs that celebrated language. Their favorite wasn't Twinkle, Twinkle, it was a song-game called "The Prettiest Little Ford," which I also learned from my dad. When I was a kid we used to sing this song on long car trips without a radio or heater during the Depression. It went like this:

> There was a little Ford,
> The cutest little Ford,
> The prettiest little Ford that you ever did see.
> The Ford was on the wheels,
> The wheels were on the ground,
> The engine in the Ford made the wheels go around.
> Match in the gas tank, boom boom!

> There was a little seat,
> The cutest little seat,
> The prettiest little seat that you ever did see.
> The seat was on the floor,
> The floor was on the wheels,
> The wheels were on the ground,
> The engine in the Ford made the wheels go around.
> Match in the gas tank, boom boom!

> There was a little hat… the hat was on the girl… etc.
> There was a little flower… the flower was on the hat… etc.
> There was a little bee… the bee was on the flower… etc.
> There was a little gnat… the gnat was on the bee… etc

And so on into absurdity or until they got so tangled up they had to stop. No one ever seemed to get tired of singing this song, though. Not even me. I wanted my kids to enjoy words as I did and as their grandfather did. Even though I had my problems with my father, he had strengths I wanted to pass down through the generations. Now my grandchildren sing "there was a little Ford" and chant "scintillate, scintillate."

Ironically, this illustrates one of the problems with language. It doesn't change much, although sometimes it needs to. English is one of the most complex languages around, with rules that often make no sense. It should be simplified, with none of this "four, fore, for" or the three ways to spell "there, their, they're" nonsense, or even "scintillate, scintillate." If I were in charge of fixing the language, I would appoint a committee of five to tweak English back into shape. I'd call them the English Overhaul Crew and the five would consist of these people (although some of them are no longer living):

- George Will, who loves big words but knows how to use them.
- William F. Buckley, who was noted for extreme pomposity.
- Allen Greenspan, who described the stock market with "irrational exuberance."
- Erma Bombeck, who wrote *The Grass Is Always Greener Over The Septic Tank.*
- Yogi Berra, who on the Aflac TV ad said, "And they'll give you cash, which is just as good as money."

And for an alternate, I'd appoint George Carlin, who would add a bit of color. Or in his case, off-color. After they were done tweaking the English language, we'd have something everyone could use.

English has become the international language of business, diplomacy and even entertainment through the popularity of Hollywood movies. English is taught as a second language in much of Europe and Asia now. Even in China, where the West has not been highly regarded, there are state-run radio programs that teach people how to speak English. The Chinese are very smart.

They know that to succeed economically, they need to speak the common language of business.

When groups of immigrants come to another country, the ones who prosper the fastest are those who speak the native language. In fact, these translators often become monarchs of their immigrant communities because everyone else is helpless when they cannot speak the dominant language of the society.

English needs to be overhauled because we need to make it easier for non-English speakers to learn how to speak it and write it. I admit that it would be hard to get a committee of five to change the language so that everyone would agree (especially since some of my committee are dead), but we need to attempt it anyway.

Why is this so important? Because we can't talk to each other, that's why! And because we can't talk to each other, we don't understand each other, and then we fight with each other. I'm convinced that if we all spoke a common language, there would be fewer wars.

This doesn't mean I think other languages should die out. That would be a great shame, as culture and language are closely tied together. We need to preserve all world cultures because they contain wisdom and beauty, as well as a historical record, that would be lost if they became extinct. Look at what happened to the Native Americans. When European settlers came to America they tried, and in many cases succeeded, to wipe out the native languages. They funneled Native American children into schools where it was forbidden to speak anything but English. What a huge mistake this was. Now some Native American tribes are trying to resurrect their cultures' languages, and since often there are only a few old people left who speak these languages, it's an immense challenge.

I think everyone on Earth should be bilingual, at the very least. Maybe even trilingual. First, everyone should speak their native language, the language of their ancestors or their

YOUR HONOR, MY CLIENT WISHES TO FILE
A MOTION FOR A CHANGE OF VENUE

homelands. Second, everyone should speak English, the internationally accepted language of diplomacy and even more importantly, trade. And third, I think everyone should also speak another widely spoken language, such as Spanish or Chinese.

This wouldn't really be so difficult to do, although it may be beyond the capacity of older folks like me. But if all countries instituted educational programs that automatically taught children three languages, it would be only a couple of generations before everyone in the world was bilingual or trilingual. And then maybe we'd try to understand each other. At least we'd have a better chance of doing so.

Chapter Ten

What Will Replace Us?

If we didn't have machines, we'd still be traveling on horseback or gathering roots and berries by hand. I appreciate machines and anything mechanical. I'm good at figuring out how things work as long as I can see the pieces, take them apart and put them back together again. It seems to come naturally to me.

But I wouldn't go so far as to say I have a "feeling" for machines or that I "understand" machinery. After all, a machine is just a machine. It has no feelings because it's not alive. If you take a gear out of a machine, it just sits there. It won't do anything until a human being puts it in its proper place and sets it in motion.

My dad wasn't mechanical. He stood in the front of a classroom all day and talked, which was what he was good at. He liked to read about machines, but as soon as he had to work with his hands he looked confused. Nevertheless, he once made an air conditioner all by himself.

We lived in Modesto, California, when I was between 10 and 13 years old. It's hot in Modesto in the summertime. The only method we had of cooling the house was a screen door, which of course was pretty useless. Dad didn't like being uncomfortable, so when he read an article in *Popular Mechanics* telling how to make something called a swamp cooler, he decided to try. He got a fan and an old washing machine motor and mounted the fan on the shaft of the motor. Then he put this contraption in a box which he packed with stuff called excelsior — long strips of wood that had the consistency of steel wool. He hooked up a water trickle bar to keep the excelsior wet and the fan whooshed the air through the dripping excelsior, cooling the air down, and then blowing it out a vent into the house.

The swamp cooler was the only mechanical thing I remember my father making, but it impressed me so much that I can recall all the steps even today. I was his helper and I learned a lot. It was fascinating for me to hear him read the instructions out loud and then turn the words into something real you could make with your hands. I could see in my mind which parts fit with other parts and how if you moved one thing it would have an effect on another. This was something my father was unable to do. I think he was going on faith in the written word and he was surprised and pleased when the swamp cooler actually cooled our house. But as soon as I heard the directions, I knew it would work. I wasn't surprised at all.

My talent with machinery came in handy making my living in the construction industry. I worked with a lot of heavy equipment and hydraulic machinery, which are full of motors, cylinders, valves, hoses and tubes all working together in perfect synchronization. Our machines were so busy that during my company's operation we wore out 19 backhoes.

But today's machines are different from what I learned and understood in the past. I got a new Dell printer and had to have it set up for me. And even then it took me 15 minutes and some swearing to learn how to send a fax. I bought an electronic toy for my granddaughter and I couldn't even understand the directions to help her set it up.

And I really don't get how a computer works. I can't take it apart and see the moving parts. I can't say, "Oh, I see how this works — this thing connects over to this other thing, and if you pull that thing this will happen." I'm used to Snap-on and Crafts-man tools, but Google and even Windows are beyond me. It's been suggested to me that it's a generational thing (a polite way of telling me that I'm too old), but I don't know. One of my sons-in-law is software engineer for Microsoft and even he says he can't explain how everything in a computer works.

The rate that machines are changing boggles my mind. I remember my mother-in-law, who was born in 1896, telling me how excited she felt when the horse-and-buggy was replaced with the automobile, and how astonished she felt the first time she rode in an airplane. When men landed on the moon she told me, "There's nothing left. I've seen it all." She died about five years later in 1974. I don't know what she would have said about the new machines that have come along since 1974. She hadn't seen it all. There was more to come.

Now I know just how she felt. Our first telephone was a wooden box on the wall and you had to turn a crank to get it to work. Two longs and a short was our ring on the party line. When we got our first radio that was a major innovation. We listened to Jack Benny and Fred Allen. My mother did her housework while listening to her favorite soap opera. That's a benefit radio had over TV — you didn't have to sit still and watch it. TV wastes a lot of time.

Now there's the internet and email. I use them some, but nothing like my children and especially my grandchildren. I don't do text messaging, although I do have a cell phone. Every time I think I'm getting used to some new technology, something else replaces it.

It's not just us who are getting smarter about using machines. The machines themselves are getting smarter. Many robots now can do the work of humans, in factories and in space. The upside to this is that it's safer and more efficient. The downside is that it's putting blue collar workers out of work. There are now smart computers which can figure out what a human is likely to input next and will anticipate their actions. Some computer robots are even designed to have built-in personality traits. I may be old-fashioned, but I find this kind of freaky.

Now we have machines telling other machines what to do, like robots running heavy machinery and coordinating assembly lines. I must admit that machines may be better at mindless tasks than humans are. We have wandering minds, and the smarter we are, the more our minds wander.

I did a lot of ditch digging in my time. It's not a demanding job — you sit on a tractor and pull levers and use about 5% of your brain. The rest of your brain is daydreaming. I used to think about stuff like space and the role of religion — the same stuff that's in this book. I wasn't focused on my work and I made mistakes.

That's why machines are useful. They don't wonder about things. They don't ask questions. They are totally focused and they always follow directions. Unless they break down of course!

I wonder if robots could be programmed to wonder and ask questions. I don't know if this is possible. Still, since robots are now being designed with "brains" and "personalities," it isn't so far-fetched to think robots may develop self-awareness someday. And isn't that one of the hallmarks we use to separate us humans from the rest of the creatures on Earth? This used to be science fiction, but who knows what will happen in another hundred years? Much of science fiction written in the 19th century came true in the 20th.

When I read Bill Gates' book *The Road Ahead*, I was comforted when he said that computers will never be able to take over for human beings. I trust Bill Gates when it comes to computers. After all, he's had a little success in that arena.

I agree with Bill Gates. I don't think robots and computers, no matter how much personality you program into them, will become self-aware, conscious beings. Even if they could wonder and ask questions, how would you program them to respond to the unexpected or the brand-new?

The bottom line is that machines need human beings to turn them on. A human has to start them up and step on the gas. Even though they are powerful and so complex that many of us can't understand how they work, they are still only tools. They respond to input, but they don't think. And because machines and computers are built by humans, they can't surpass the intelligence of the humans who create them. So I don't think we'll be replaced by machines, at least not anytime soon.

Chapter Eleven

Can We Keep This Up?

The answer to this chapter's title is: *not much longer.*

The human race is approaching extinction. The earth itself will be habitable for another two billion years or so before it dies of natural causes, but unless we change the way we are using its resources there will be no humans here to inhabit it during those two billion years. Cockroaches are said to be able to survive almost anything — maybe they'll be here with the ants and mosquitoes, but we won't be.

I know this is a book of questions, but there really is no question about this: if we don't learn to rein in our excesses, we will exterminate ourselves. We are recklessly squandering the future availability of what natural resources still remain, and we haven't yet come to the realization that we have more to worry about than military annihilation. We humans lay claim to the notion of being the most intelligent of all species, but if we're so smart why aren't we taking better care of our habitat?

We are as confined to this planet as animals in a zoo. We depend completely on our environment to sustain ourselves. Everything we have or ever will have is here. And we are consuming it at such an alarming rate that we can actually see the end approaching. I'm not talking thousands of years to figure out what to do — we'll be lucky if we have a few hundred. That means my grandchildren may breathe their last breaths as the rest of humanity dies with them. They may witness their children living — and dying — in unimaginable discomfort. Perhaps their last moments will be filled with screaming panic or the whimpers of abandonment. Do you want this for your grandchildren? I know I don't want it for mine.

I'm not a doomsayer or a naturally gloomy person. I try to stay on the side of optimism. This is getting increasingly hard to do. Less than 200 years ago we found a use for oil as a fuel in lamps, and then a short time later we found we could fuel machines with oil. Then we used it to pave roads and parking lots, and then we found we could make it into plastics. It exploded from there. Now petroleum is in nearly everything we consume. It's not just cars guzzling all the oil.

Oil isn't like trees. We can't plant it. We can't make more. It is a finite resource. When it's gone, it's gone. We are drilling now as deep as seven miles down and are pumping several million barrels of oil daily. A barrel holds 42 gallons. That's a lot of oil, and there is no possibility of replacing it. How much deeper can we go? Not much deeper, and even if we could soon there will be nothing there, no matter how deep we drill.

But perhaps we'll be gone before the oil is gone, since we're now engaged in fighting and killing each other over the dwindling pockets of oil around the world.

If you are a North American, as I am, you might be ashamed to learn that we produce 5% of the world's output of oil, yet we consume 20%. This is scary enough, but soon China and India will outpace even our demand. China has already surpassed our energy consumption.

This probably isn't news to you, if you've been paying attention at all during the last few years. Most of us finally agree that we have a problem, but of course we can't agree on what to do about it. Yet there are a lot of ideas out there. Maybe some of them would work.

I remember many years ago, probably around 1960, talking to a traffic engineer who had envisioned a magnetic coupler system for cars and trucks. He was concerned, even back then, about reducing consumption of oil, although his reason was more financial than environmental. His job included flying around in an airplane over traffic and studying traffic patterns. Traffic tends to surge as cars try to get up to speed, as they enter and exit the roadway, and as drivers try to maintain a safe distance between themselves and other vehicles. The engineer's idea was rather than build new roads, we should develop a system where everybody was coupled together, like a train. From the air, you wouldn't see the surging. It would look like a swarm of bees moving together down a roadway. There were a lot more details, but the end result was that it would save a lot of fuel. Who knows if

NO, IT DOESN'T FLY. IT'S AN ELECTRIC CAR THAT YOU DON'T HAVE TO PLUG IN.

something like that could even work, but it was certainly a creative solution.

Reducing our use of oil is only going to be possible if we develop other sources of energy. Solar activity is free. The sun is throwing all its energy out there in all directions and it will keep on doing it until it expires in a few billion years. If we can collect it for nothing, why don't we? Wind is free too. So are rain and snow. It means developing a new infrastructure and demolishing the old one, which means time and money, but we really have no choice.

And I haven't even mentioned the environmental damage we are doing to the earth through our overuse of oil. Our air and our soil and our water are polluted, making it dangerous to breathe, eat and drink. When I was a teenager in Berkeley, California, I used to ride my bike up Grizzly Peak Boulevard to the top of the hills overlooking San Francisco Bay. There were days when the smog was so bad that you couldn't see the Golden Gate Bridge, only 15 miles away. My eyes would be stinging when I got back home. And this was in the 1940s!

I don't mean to preach. Years ago, I was no better than any other North American in terms of squandering resources and trashing the earth. I remember when the atomic tests were being conducted in the late 1940s. One fact that sticks in my mind was that if a nuclear chain reaction occurred during the Bikini Atoll blasting, the entire ocean could evaporate. I don't remember anyone being too concerned about this. The mindset at the time was that it was just the ocean, as if the ocean didn't matter. Same thing when we did testing in the desert of Alamogordo, New Mexico — if there were negative consequences, it was just the desert, after all. Years later many of the observers of these tests came down with major medical complications. Those were the cream of scientific minds. This same level of genius in later years created Agent Orange. Now we have "smart" bombs.

I'm sorry I didn't teach my kids better respect for the earth when they were growing up. I had to learn it first. I was a little slow to catch up. I don't remember much about the environmental movement of the 1970s, for instance. I was busy working, building my business, which was directly tied to land development. Luckily my kids did learn, with or without my help.

It wasn't until the last decade that I've become aware of the looming threat to the earth. I've always been a science nut and the more I read the more concerned I became. But the real tipping point came in an atypical way for me. I've been a lifelong Republican and I've never trusted Democrats much. They always want to give away too much of my hard-earned money. But right after the movie *An Inconvenient Truth* came out, my youngest daughter came to visit. One night she rented this movie and we watched it together. I guess you could say that movie, and Al Gore himself, blew me away. He did two things — he explained what was happening in layman's terms and he offered hope — if we would only get off our butts and do something. What a movie. I even forgave Gore for being a Democrat.

What Al Gore did for me was not only increase my knowledge, but he raised my awareness. And that is what I think is needed, if we wish to survive. We need awareness. We cannot bury our heads in the sand anymore. We have to take them out and look around. And when we see that something needs to be done, we can't push it off on the next generation. We may be the last generation that has a chance to do something before it's too late.

We have a responsibility to the generations that come after us. There's an Iroquois teaching that says, "In our every deliberation, we must consider the impact of our decisions on the next seven generations." You honor your ancestors by your actions and your words, and you protect your descendants in the same way. This is the order of the universe and we need to work within that order. We can't order nature to suit ourselves.

Each of our individual actions matter! What you do and say has consequences. This means we can't blame the world's problems on those who came before us. And we can't shrug in defeat and say, "It's too big a problem and I'm just one little person." This isn't true. If each of us did something, things would change.

Chapter Twelve

Who Owns What?

Private property is one of the things Americans believe in. I believe in it too. After all, I own property. Since I sold my construction company, managing my properties is how I earn my living.

At the same time, it's pretty silly to think that we humans can really own the land. Actually we are stewards, taking care of the land, improving it or protecting it. And there are times when we have to act together, in spite of individual property rights, or the earth pays too big a price.

We moved around California a lot when I was a kid. My parents didn't own any land of their own. My first memories are from the Depression, when we lived in Hickman. There's a photograph of me and my sister in 1932 standing in front of the chicken house we lived in. My father was out of work, having lost his job at Modesto High School right before they would have had to give him tenure. Somebody, I'm not sure who, gave our family free use of their chicken house, otherwise we would have had nowhere to live. My parents took the roosts out and cleaned the droppings out with a square point shovel. My mother got down on her hands and knees and scrubbed the wooden floor with

Clorox. She made curtains out of chicken-meal sacks. I was only five at the time, but it's something I remember clearly.

My younger sister and me in front of our chicken house.
August, 1932. Hickman, California.

The following year we rented a cabin in Modesto for $15 a month, while Dad worked as a fig picker. He earned 50¢ a lug. A lug was about 50 pounds of fruit in a wooden box. After Modesto we moved to Escalon for another year or so and then we moved to a small town called Linden, population 150. Dad got a high school teaching job there for $150 a month; I attended a three room grammar school. His teaching salary was almost enough to keep us, but he also had a job as a fruit buyer for a dry yard during summer vacation too. I remember the house we lived in, we rented it for $35 a month.

We moved again when I was in fourth or fifth grade, back to Modesto. Dad got another teaching position so he had a steady job, but he still didn't own any property. I have another memory of riding my bike home from grammar school when I was around 10 or 11, and seeing a "For Sale" sign on a one-acre lot at the edge of town. They wanted $150 for it. When I got home I told my dad about it, I think because I wanted him to buy it. I was probably tired of moving around and thought if we owned property we could stay where we were. We were sitting at the kitchen table when I mentioned it. He pushed himself out of his chair, leaned across the table and poked his finger in my face. "Anybody who's crazy enough to spend a month's salary on a piece of land outside of town," he said, "ought to be put in the Stockton Mental Institution."

Fifty years later I reminded him of this conversation. He shrugged and said, "California only had a population of about five million in the whole state back then. Now there's twice that many in the Bay Area alone. And it's growing."

Now nearly all the property in America is owned by humans. The American West is supposed to be the land of big open spaces, but there aren't many of them left. Even the ones that are, somebody owns them; if not privately owned, they are publicly owned. It started over a hundred years ago with the railroads. The railroads were awarded a free square mile on alternate sections down the right of way of any railroad they laid. Wherever they had a service spot for their engines became a station, and then a town. Even today there are vast holdings still in railroads' hands. It's virtually impossible to buy any of their land because they know how much it's worth. They run one engine a month just to maintain a right of way and thus keep the land. In my opinion these laws need attention.

Owning and developing land is fenced in by government regulations, many of which don't make sense and will just about drive you bonkers. I agree that we need some regulations, but why not make sensible ones? Then maybe there wouldn't be so much disagreement and fighting over property lines.

No one in my family was a property owner until the 1950s. During the Depression my aunt and uncle and my two cousins, Gordon and Margaret, lived about 300 miles from us in Corning, California. They were even poorer than we were; our chicken house was a palace compared to how they lived. My aunt told me that one winter they lived off of approximately a 100-pound sack of cornmeal, and that was it. They had cornmeal pancakes, cornmeal mush and cornmeal muffins, for breakfast, lunch and dinner every day. Maybe that winter was what made my cousin Gordon such a driven man. He was the person who got me into owning and developing properties.

Gordon might have started out land and money poor, but he didn't end up that way. He started and ran an architectural firm, even though he wasn't a licensed architect himself. He was a wheeler-dealer, at a time when wheeling and dealing was a good thing, not a bad one. He knew what he was doing. He put together a family partnership to buy land and offered me one-sixth of it. We purchased 480 acres for $52,000 with a down payment of $15,000. Two years later we sold every bit of it for $168,000. It was a good deal then and sounds unbelievable today.

The only problem was that when we ran the required survey to subdivide the land, a question arose over where the property lines were. The last survey had been a National Geographic survey done in 1876. The benchmark monuments in California are Mount Whitney, Mount Diablo and Mount Shasta. All surveys are drawn from those points, but our property bench marks were piles of rocks and "witness trees." From 1876! In the early 1960s when we had the survey updated, there was a county road supposedly along the edge of our parcel. But it turned out that the road was 40 feet off on one end and another 40 feet off in the other direction on the other end. We had to get quitclaim deeds reciprocated with the affected land to realign it with the actual road. It was a complicated mess, but worth it in the long run. We subdivided the land into 48 pieces, 10 acres each. Years later I met a man who bought one of those 10-acre pieces and he told me he sold it for over $100,000. When you think that we bought it for $108 an acre, that's a pretty good return on investment.

Government regulation has gotten worse since then. When Lucy and I bought a building in 1988 we were promised a sewer by the city — in the future. After a few years the city finally put in the sewer, but then they demanded that to connect to it we would have to go through 600 feet of someone else's property. Why? Because they had rezoned our property in the meantime. And if the other property owner didn't want to let me go through his property, I'd be sunk. Which I was, because he didn't. Three years later I was able to access the sewer through a different property, but I got lucky. Government has gotten way too complicated. Why can't we make it simpler?

As much as I hate government regulation, I know there's a place for it. For one thing, we need to protect the environment. We can't have developers going hog-wild and raping the environment just to build inferior-quality houses that they sell to people who can't afford them. The countryside will disappear and the urban areas will spread like a big ooze over the land. However, tying up 23 million acres of national rainforest hasn't done much for the endangered spotted owl. But its impact on the lumber industry has been horrific.

And then we must look at natural disasters. Some of them can be prevented and others can be predicted and protections put in place, if the government will take charge and efficiently do things about them. Take earthquakes, for example. Some people say we shouldn't build on earthquake faults, but I think that's nonsense. Just about every place is on an earthquake fault. I have a copy of

THE DILEMMA OF THE SPOTTED OWL

the January 1973 issue of *National Geographic*, which had a global map of all the recorded earthquakes in the world. The only area on the map that showed as earthquake-free was Australia. And in the next decade there was a horrendous earthquake there. A geologist once told me that you are within 15 miles of a possible major earthquake fault no matter where you live. You don't have to live in San Francisco on the San Andreas Fault to be vulnerable. So we can't prevent them. But the government mandates earthquake bracing into building codes that will reduce the effect that earthquakes might have.

A great example of the difference between man-made and natural disasters is the mess surrounding Hurricane Katrina in 2005. You can argue about whether Katrina was man-made or not; many people think global warming contributed to it. Maybe it did, but hurricanes have been around a lot longer than we have. Perhaps building in a low-lying place like New Orleans was a mistake too. That started with the French settlers, or maybe even earlier; maybe Native American tribes lived there and were wiped out periodically by the hurricanes that bedevil that area.

And then after they built the settlement, maybe they shouldn't have diked it up. But if they did dike it up, then maybe they should have made sure the dikes would hold. And finally, they sure as hell should have had a plan to evacuate the people, or at least to get supplies to the survivors. What a mess, and most of it could have been prevented if the people owning that property had behaved intelligently, or if the government had regulations to make them.

Wildfires and how we handle them is another matter we should look at. In California we have horrendous fires every year, running into millions of acres and billions of dollars lost. In the construction industry they pay exorbitant prices for lumber partly because of this. But much of this could be prevented if forestry methods were improved. Who should do this? Whoever owns the property, that's who. In some cases this is the government, in others private landowners. Both of them are affected by politics. Even though there's been a lot of research into how to prevent fires, such as the proper planting of ground cover or establishing firebreaks every five miles in all directions, no one can seem to agree on how to manage our forests. All we do is fight over what to do and millions of trees go up in flames.

A related subject is water and how we handle that. Seems like every couple of years we have droughts. We should be used to them by now and know how to handle them. I've been involved in building for most of my life and I've seen how stupid we are when it comes to water and development. If I had my way, any new building developments going in would be required to put in wells to supply the irrigation to water the lawns and shrubbery. Why are we using processed water for that? There is more fluoridated water flowing into my lawn in one day than I use in brushing my teeth in one year. The outside water, including the outside hose bibs, should be fed off a well system, one well for the whole housing tract. The water would be cheap to obtain and wouldn't drain down the processed water to a point where we keep shouting "Drought!" Most of irrigation water absorbs into the ground and contributes to the water table which is the source for water wells.

The bigger question of property rights is beyond American borders, or any borders. We are increasingly realizing that all the humans on the earth are in this together. We all live on the same planet. What happens in San Francisco affects Beijing, and what happens in Rio de Janeiro affects Paris. The question of how to handle national sovereignty is a tough one to answer. Do we have the right to tell Brazil what to do about their rainforests? They're cutting them down at an alarming rate, so they can make room for grazing lands for cattle, or to grow the grain to feed the cattle, so they can sell the meat to beef-addicted countries like the United States. Not only are the rainforests disappearing (and we don't really understand yet the full ramifications of this), but the methane gasses given off by the cattle's digestive systems is just as big a cause of pollution as cars. But even though this problem is shared by everyone on Earth, no one except the Brazilians has the authority to stop cutting down the rainforest. What's the answer to this? I don't know.

I just wish we didn't have to be so possessive about land. Not everyone is. Here in California we live on a modest lot with a fence around it. Where my wife's relatives live back in Pennsylvania there are no fences anywhere. They have lawns, as we do here, but they don't "protect" them from each other. They say, "While you're gone, I'll mow your lawn, Charlie. When I'm gone, you'll mow mine." I think I prefer that kind of cooperation to competition. Like the narrator in Robert Frost's poem *Mending Fences*, I'm not convinced that "good fences make good neighbors."

I don't know which proportion of public to private ownership is correct. I guess we have to keep trying until we get it right. Although I'm not so sure we'll ever get it right, no matter how hard we try. What we should aim for is getting it better than it is. Maybe that would be enough.

Chapter Thirteen

How Many Is Too Many?

Our planet is not getting any larger and never will. New land is not appearing before our eyes. Our resources are being used at an unsustainable rate. And yet we humans are multiplying faster and dying slower than ever before.

We can't go on like this. We not only have to control our population, we have to reduce it. The only way to do this is to decrease the birth rate or increase the death rate. Unfortunately, we seem to be doing the exact opposite.

The huge Baby Boomer generation, about 80 million people in the US alone, is now in late middle age and before long will be old. Most of them might live well into their 80s or beyond, due to improved medical technology. But then they'll be gone and our population will be under control again, right? Wrong! Because the Baby Boomers' children, the so-called Millennial generation, is just as big as, or bigger than their parents' generation. And who knows what we'll call their children. But you can bet there will be a lot of them.

Everyone assumes that living a long life is a good thing. Which it is in many ways. But we are holding human life so precious that we're trying to stretch our life expectancy to well above a hundred — in fact some scientists say that humans may well live to 120 and beyond in the next century. That means old people are going to be taking up a lot of room. But what about the room needed for the young, the children, the babies? Don't they get any?

Don't get me wrong. I'm all for the advancements in medical science. Without them, I wouldn't be here. I've had three different kinds of cancer, at three different times. The first was in 1991 at age 64. I had a form of leukemia known as hairy cell (because that's what it looks like under a microscope). It's a rare form of cancer, only about 600 cases a year in the US. My oncologist put an IV in my arm that went down to a pump on my belt. The IV ran up to my jugular vein. I walked around with this thing for exactly 168 hours, or one solid week. I was cured.

Next I had prostate cancer in 2005. I had laparoscopic surgery to have my prostate removed, and because I'm not in the propagating business anymore, I elected not to have hormone or chemotherapy. My prostate may be gone, but so is the cancer.

The third cancer was skin cancer in 2008. I got a lump on the back of my hand. It kept getting bigger and more tender. I went to the dermatologist and he took it off. He sent it to the lab and it came back as malignant. But we got it all, so I'm skin cancer free too. But we're still watching it. My father died of a melanoma and he suffered terribly. He was dependent on morphine for the last eight months of his life. I don't want to go like him.

Meanwhile, my wife Lucy had breast cancer in 2002 and even my youngest daughter had it in 2006. Lucy eventually died of cancer, but her initial treatment gave her an additional eight years. Medical science saved their lives too.

So I've had a lot of experience with illness and getting old. I had a brain scan a couple of years ago. They told me I had the "normal amount of brain calcification for a man my age." Brain calcification, great.

But I don't get all stressed over it. I'm over 80, it's to be expected. Disease is all over, a part of our lives. Impurities are in our food, the air we breathe, the water we drink. Why should I sit here and fret about it? I'm going to deal with it and move on with my life. I like my life. I like to live. But if I don't move on, then I'll move out and finally find out what comes next. Who knows, maybe it will be interesting.

I'm not afraid to die. The older I get, the more this is true. I think it's true for a lot of us. Mostly what we're afraid of is becoming a drooling vegetable, or a burden on our kids, or imprisoned in a nursing home because we can't take care of ourselves. Or worse, living with hopeless pain like my wife Lucy did. I think we have a right to end our own lives if it's truly hopeless. I know there are those who say this is wrong, a sin against life. The ones saying that aren't old yet. I bet they change their tune when they are.

Yeah, I'd like to live to 120 if I could feel as I do now. At the same time, I don't think it's fair to those replacements coming up. What's the answer? I don't know.

Now there *are* some answers to the questions posed by the other half of this problem — how do we decrease the birth rate? At first glance, it seems to be a pretty easy answer. We know how to control reproduction. So why don't we? Politics and religion again, leading to disagreements. Not only do we disagree on how to control reproduction, we disagree on whether we should.

Arguments on whether we should control reproduction tend to center on contraception, sterilization and abortion — all of them political hot buttons. People's faces turn red. They start to yell. They pass laws and break laws, and they even throw bombs at each other. This is ridiculous. We are an intelligent species with brains. We need to use our brains to have rational discussions about the options we have open to us. Otherwise it won't matter what side you are on. All sides will lose.

In China they tried to solve the overpopulation problem by government mandate, making it illegal to have more than one child. To Americans, that sounds like an abuse of human rights, an insult to personal freedom. And in China it led to the abandonment and murder of baby girls, because of the preference for boy babies in their culture. When those boy babies grew up, where were they going to find women to marry if so many of the baby girls were dropped down wells? I don't think forced family planning is the answer. In some countries where the birth rate has dropped, like Japan and France, the government gives tax incentives to couples having a third child. I think that's nuts. It would be more to the point if the government gave tax incentives to having less than two children. Or gave tax incentives to people who got themselves sterilized. What does it matter if the children are French, American, Chinese, or African? We all live on the same Planet Earth.

Let's think about sterilization. Vasectomies and tubal ligations are fairly easy procedures, carrying little risk. We neuter our dogs and cats to control their population, why not do the same for humans? We could sterilize criminals, especially sexual criminals.

We could license parenting. You have to have a license to drive a car, why not have a license to become a parent?

I think the real answer is education. My wife Lucy was a social worker in some of the poorest communities in the Bay Area. She saw little girls, no more than 13 or 14, become pregnant again and again just because they didn't know how to stop it. What chance did their children have? Yet you couldn't even offer them tubal ligation, because that would be trampling on their civil rights.

And I'm not even going to get into abortion. That can of worms turns normally reasonable people into raving lunatics. I wish we could just have a rational discussion.

To my mind the big downside to controlling birth is the danger that we'll end up controlling what kind of people we allow to be born. We have the science to do it now. Maybe there would be laws passed saying you couldn't have a baby who had a genetic disability, or even a potential disability. Think about that for a minute. Some of the most creative, out-of-the-box thinkers have been "different." It's widely believed that even Einstein had dyslexia, a learning disability. Overcoming disabilities often leads to courage and insight. Do we want to lose that?

We've done it with dogs. We selected for docility, so they could be more easily trained. Now they're not wolves any longer. We could likewise remake the human race into a homogenous, bland race of conformists. Probably no war, but no imagination either. No new ideas. No music, no art. That's pretty scary. This is exactly what Hitler and Stalin attempted to do before and during World War II, and we all know how horrifying that was.

The bottom line is there are no perfect answers to the question of what to do about overpopulation — at least there are no answers we've found yet that will satisfy everybody. There are upsides and downsides to everything. It's important to see both. Otherwise we don't have a prayer of knowing what to do about the challenges we face.

I think of what's going on in my own family right now. My youngest daughter chose not to have children of her own. She and her husband adopted. They not only adopted, they adopted older kids, not babies. I'm proud of her, of course. When she first told me about their plans, though, I wondered how I'd feel about those kids. Would it be the same as with my other grandchildren, the ones who are blood related to me? Maybe not, but is that bad? No, it's just different. My daughter tells me that adoption is one way of slowing overpopulation. Rather than giving birth to new children, adoption gives a home to children who are already here and need a family. I'm sure she's right. I'm glad she adopted those kids. I want them in the family.

Chapter Fourteen

Follow the Leader?

Leadership is a valued quality. Sometimes we follow our leaders with zest and sometimes with reluctance. But most of us need to follow someone. We must have leaders, because without them we get lost. Who the leaders follow is another question.

Throughout history there have been good leaders and bad leaders. Many times we've had flat-out evil and dangerous leaders. For an example, look at Genghis Khan. Loyalty was everything to him — that and intimidating his enemies any way he could. I read somewhere that to illustrate to his enemies how loyal his troops were he would actually order a couple of lines of troops to march over a cliff to their certain deaths. Which they did. If they hadn't marched off the cliff they would have been killed anyway, but many of them evidently marched willingly, proud to prove their loyalty. It seems like insanity not only for the troops who died, but for Genghis Khan himself. After all, those troops were a valuable part of his property. But he was willing to use them as tools to demoralize his enemies. It worked, too. His enemies were often scared to death, literally.

What makes people follow power-crazed madmen like Genghis Khan? I don't think it's that hard to figure out. People are motivated by fear, greed, or love. Anyone who promises you riches — in the form of loot from the enemy, whoever that may be — is going to be popular. Anyone who guarantees your safety — even if it's safety in Heaven and not on Earth — is going to be followed. Anyone who holds your family hostage, promising that if you don't do what he says your kids will starve — is going to be obeyed. Anyone who makes you believe that the "other guy" is coming right now to kill you and your mother and your children and even your God — is going to get you to fight for him.

It's no good saying that Genghis Khan lived a long time ago and we don't act like that anymore, because we do. The power hungry have been around forever and they're still here. Wars cannot be fought without them. From the Vikings to the Crusaders to the Nazis, they were able to do so much damage because they had leaders who were able to manipulate, inspire, or coerce people into obedience. In my lifetime alone I can easily think of three evil men who followed in Genghis Khan's footsteps — Adolf Hitler, Josef Stalin and Osama bin Laden. Oh I left out Tojo, the chief architect of kamikaze suicide bombings.

Only today the stakes are so much higher than they've ever been before. Genghis Khan couldn't blow up a continent and murder literally millions of people at once. He didn't have weapons that would poison the land and the oceans and the air for generations. He also couldn't strap explosives on women or children and send them into crowded marketplaces to blow themselves up. Maybe he wasn't that evil, we don't know. But we do know that there are plenty of people in our time who are. Nothing, no cruelty or barbarism, is off-limits and their resources for destruction may be unlimited — if they can get their hands on them. But the scariest thing about them is the same thing that made Genghis Khan so scary — they get other people to follow their lead. They are leaders.

So am I saying we should do away with all leaders? No. Without leaders, all we'd have is chaos and anarchy. The one thing that human beings cannot live without is order. So we've got to have leaders; we just have to be careful in choosing them. We cannot allow ourselves to be swayed by fear, greed, or love. Instead of emotion, we need to use our heads.

99

That's why I believe democracy, particularly American democracy, is the best system we've developed so far. We have leaders, but they are not tyrants. We have a system for getting rid of leaders who don't lead us in the right direction.

I am a proud American, so maybe I'm prejudiced. It's easy to get caught up in blind patriotism, but I don't believe I am a blind patriot. I know the United States isn't perfect. This is especially true of our modern government. I believe that government nowadays is way too complex and full of bureaucratic nonsense. At the same time, I know there are things that only government can do.

The irony is that it would be simpler to have one unquestioned leader, a dictator whose every word is law. That would be simple: you either obey him or you and your family die or live in squalor. Because democracy has checks and balances levied on our leaders, and we choose our leaders ourselves, we are free of that tyranny. But those checks and balances and voting rights also create the bureaucracy and thicket of tangled laws that are strangling us.

We are imposing more and more political control over every aspect of our lives. For example, the IRS code is estimated to be 66,000 pages long — or more. No one person can know all of it and the majority can't understand any of it. And yet "ignorance of the law is no excuse" and violators of this code can be fined or imprisoned for years.

When Hillary Clinton was first lady and working on that health plan of hers, I sent her a letter explaining my idea for a simpler plan than the one she was proposing. About two or three months later I got a form letter from the White House that basically said "Thanks, but no thanks." Probably the only one who read my plan was some intern.

My proposal for a simpler health plan would work quite well today. It doesn't look to the government to pay everything — in the end, we are the government. We'll pay for everything anyway. I think we should base health care insurance on what the government did with GI life insurance during World War II. When I was in the Navy, they gave us $10,000 worth of term life insurance. In actuarial tables we were a big risk — we were at war. It cost $6.25 a month or 12.5% of our salary. A pretty big chunk when you only make $50 a month as an apprentice seaman. But on the other hand, who else would insure us? The government was in the position to take on this risk for GIs. We should offer voluntary coverage to the entire medical profession where the premium is based on breaking even, which is what the GI deal was. It was an effective program. My plan would have a 10% deductible premium and would be based on existing actuary tables. Existing insurance companies and the legal profession could fill in the 10%. Then the medical professionals could better practice medicine. Our current administration recently passed a new health care plan, but at this point I'm not sure how it compares to my own plan. Until it's put into practice none of us will really know how it will play out.

Trying to change anything in the government now is all but impossible. That's because of politics. Nothing is simple; anything one candidate says is sure to be challenged by the other party and opens up a can of worms. The worms get out and slither all over the place and all we can do is to try to corral them again and stuff them back in the can. That's a good description of an election year. It's insane that in the case of the president, it takes two years to run for a four year office. How can he (or she) lead, if he's always trying to save his job?

Elephants have long memories and we need to pin the tail on the liberal Donkey. Emphasis is on the wrong end of the animal. As Republicans, we need to protect the healthcare industry from too much litigation and limit excessive lawsuits. Let the medical world practice medicine without the catastrophically expensive insurance costs in many of the sensitive areas of medicine, such as brain surgery, cancer treatment — you name it!

Here I am again, raising questions that I can't answer. I don't know the answer on how to restructure government so it's less complicated. I don't know how to pick our leaders in a better way. The only thing I'm pretty sure of is that we need to talk to each other sensibly without getting stuck in our own ruts, unable to see over the fences that we ourselves have erected. We need to seek the middle ground so we can achieve the things that are possible and look to the government to help us. Sometimes it must be mandated, if people aren't freely willing to do it themselves. How do you find the balance?

No, I don't have the answers, just questions. But I think if we keep asking questions and proposing solutions (without being married to them), more ideas would be generated. People's awareness would be heightened. Perhaps our famous critical-thinking abilities would at last kick in and we would elect leaders who will show us the way forward.

Chapter Fifteen

Why War?

War is group insanity. Nearly everyone agrees with this; only the megalomaniacs think war is a good idea. (And you'll notice that the warmongers are hardly ever in the thick of battle themselves.) Then why do we have wars? This is a good question, one that has been asked over and over for thousands of years and never answered.

We keep using our brightest innovators to create ever more destructive weapons. Starting from clubs we progressed to spears, then bows and arrows, then guns, then bombs. In the modern world we've gone from fission to fusion to cobalt munitions and there is no end in sight. We've made it possible to kill many more people at once and we've made it physically and emotionally easier on the killers — you no longer have to club someone over the head and have him bleed on you, now you can lob a bomb from an airplane or a missile onto the defenseless people below. Weaponry has reached the point now that we're all aware we have the ability to blow up the entire planet. Not only can we exterminate ourselves, but blast every creature, plant and even rock that lives here into a billion tiny pieces. Our delivery systems are now on the brink of laser delivery, essentially an attack at the speed of light. There is no reflex action possible against this kind of knockout blow.

Well, look at us, aren't we smart.

I think it all comes down to competition — the desire to be on top. (Too bad we seldom ask the related question, "on top of what?") Maybe competition is built into our nature. Look at our addiction to sports. I'm not against sports; it can be good, clean fun and can teach us how to work together as well as how to beat the other guy. But competition has a downside. It can make us literally lose our minds. We act like idiots. People holding huge foam rubber fingers stating "We're number one!" wave them in the faces of others wearing hats shaped like cheese. All of them screaming obscenities at each other while they watch gladiators move a ball a yard or two, down a field of mud. If their particular gladiators don't win, fans have been known to rush the stadium and cause a riot. Does this sound like rational behavior to you?

The gladiators themselves aren't any better. They rip apart their bodies and get old before their time; they ingest dangerous drugs to inflate their strength even though they're harmed in the long run. All so they can wear a fancy ring or put a trophy on their mantle; so they can say "I won!" Won what?

Despite all that, sports are a relatively benign form of competition. They put formal boundaries around our need to be better than the next guy. It would be great if we could say we channel our competitiveness into sports instead of other forms of aggression such as war. But we don't, do we?

For millennia we have taught our children how to compete with each other. We've drawn lines between us and divided us according to our family, our team, our community, our country, our allies — and any family, team, community, country or ally on the other side of that line is our enemy.

The boundaries that we drew up years ago and now defend to the death have no reality of their own. They are imaginary, every single one of them. Our human-inspired political boundaries are ignored by all other life forms. One example is how we are ingrained with flag loyalty. Conquerors vanquish the natives of one place and then claim it for another place, and to prove it they stick a flag in the ground. We paint markings on military vehicles as symbols of how we got the best of the other guy. We talk about "our" waters off "our coasts" as if any one group of people can own the ocean. We've stuck the American flag in Antarctica like this means something. Do we think the penguins belong to us now? We plant the American flag on the moon and say, "We were here first." So what? Don't the French or the Egyptians or the Indonesians still "own" the moon too? Why do we get so caught up in allegiance to a piece of colored linen hanging on a pole?

What if there were no borders? No customs officials, no fences or moats or barriers of any kind? What are those for, anyway? Aren't they ways to keep people apart instead of bringing them together? Yes, I know there would have to be new laws and new ways to levy taxes, and most of all new ways of thinking about the ideas of nationality, culture, or country. So what? Just because ideas are new doesn't mean they are necessarily bad. At the very least I think we need to ask these questions. We've got to do something to stop us fighting and killing each other.

For one thing, loosening the borders between countries might promote travel, and nothing broadens your outlook and increases understanding of other cultures as much as visiting different places. My wife Lucy and I traveled a lot, all over the world. We went to China, Egypt, Israel, Central and Western Europe, and all over the US, even up to Alaska. It's a lot different from reading about those far-off places in the press. We watched and talked to the people on the streets, working in the restaurants and shops, traveling to work. I didn't see a whole lot of difference between them and us.

People are afraid that without borders, all "those people" would come into our country and take our jobs and take advantage of our social programs. But this is a nation made of immigrants. Unless you're Native American, you or your ancestors came here uninvited — many of them illegally. We simply have to find a civilized way to allow people to come to America (or anywhere else) and ply their trades and become good citizens. I employed a lot of people originally from Mexico and they were the same as everyone else — some of them were great workers, others not so hot. I never employed anyone illegally; I always worked within the system. But I saw a lot of hardworking people who got trampled by the system too, for no good reason that I could see.

Maybe we should ask ourselves if the concept of national boundaries has outlived its usefulness. We're all citizens of one Earth. We're going to live together or die together. We can compete with each other, sure, and sing the Star Spangled Banner at baseball games, but let's do it without guns in our hands.

The people of my generation know about war. We lived through the biggest war of all time — at least the biggest so far. War is not glorious. It is ugly, even those wars that seem justified, like World War II in which we defeated two enemies intent on murdering a big chunk of the world's people and enslaving most of the rest. The Germans slaughtered millions and plundered Europe, and the Japanese, a culture that glorified war at the time, did the same with China and other Asian neighbors. I walked the docks of Shanghai after the war and I swear you could almost see the ghosts of the murdered. It was spooky. No, the Germans and the Japanese had to be stopped and war was probably the only way — after it had gotten to that point. Why we all let it get to that point is another question.

During most of the war I was a teenager living in California, so the war in the Pacific was what I paid most attention to. It seemed closer than Europe. Like everyone else who was alive then, I remember December 7, 1941, perfectly. I was playing touch football with my buddies on Delaware Street in Berkeley. We had taken over the street and when a car came along we just moved out of the way until it passed — there was nothing like the traffic we have now. While we were playing, a kid ran out of his house onto his front porch and yelled, "They bombed Pearl Harbor! The Japs bombed Pearl Harbor!"

We all stopped playing and looked at each other. I said, "Where in the world is Pearl Harbor?"

I found out in a hurry. That night I had to go into the hospital because I got a raging secondary infection in my eczema-ridden hands. By the time I was checked in to Merritt Hospital, they already had boarded up all the windows with plywood. We had to drive to the hospital without headlights because the blackout was already imposed. Nobody knew what was going to happen. Maybe the Japanese were going to blitz us, like the Germans had done to London and Europe.

Everyone was panicked. It didn't matter that Berlin and London are only hundreds of miles apart, compared to thousands of miles between Tokyo and San Francisco. There was no way that Japanese planes could travel that far in a surprise raid, yet speculation ran rampant that the Japanese aircraft carriers were on their way to the California coast right then. Sitting in my hospital bed, my hands wrapped in bandages, I could see the frantic fear in the nurses' eyes. I felt pretty frantic myself.

After the war, everyone said that what we did to Japanese-Americans was awful — and it was. But fear makes people do things they wouldn't normally do. Entire families were rounded up and sent away to relocation camps. As an adult I sometimes wonder what happened to them, though at the time I didn't. I was only 14 and there were many things that confused me at that time. The way the Japanese disappeared was just one of them.

During high school I hoped the war would be over before I was 18, but it kept dragging on. I knew I'd have to join the service; the problem was I couldn't see myself picking up a rifle and killing someone. I couldn't even kill fish, for God's sake. And the thought of fighting hand-to-hand combat against someone armed with a bayonet terrified me. Plus I read how the Japanese bayonets were about three to four inches longer than American bayonets, which seemed to give an unfair advantage to the Japanese. When I tell this story to my family, they don't want to believe me. "You're not a coward," they say. But the truth is I was afraid.

I never considered trying to get out of serving my country. For one thing, I knew I would be drafted as soon as I turned 18 and I thought I'd be better off if I chose my branch of the service rather than letting the government do it. So four days before my 18th birthday, in January 1945, I enlisted in the Navy Reserves.

The idea of hand-to-hand combat didn't sit
well with me, so I joined the Navy.

I was still in boot camp when the war ended in Europe in May of '45. After that, we all knew it was just a matter of time before we would beat Japan — well, we may have known it, but the Japanese didn't share our opinion. Victory over Japan wasn't declared until September, so in the early fall of 1945 I was shipped out as a replacement and boarded a sub chaser in Shanghai.

I was lucky. The closest I came to military combat was with a school of whales. I was still in training and we were on a sonar training cruise off the coast of Mexico: four minelayers, which were wooden-hulled ships, and one submarine. I was on one of the minelayers. One night I was on the mid watch, which was from midnight to 0400, manning the sound gear. Around 0330 in the morning I was alerted by a series of beeps that the sonar was definitely picking up a target. The order was to call the officer of the day. So we bailed him out of the sack and he came up top side. He took one look and said, "Get on the DRT, son." (Dead Reckoning Tracer.) Then he sounded general quarters. Soon we had guys up on deck setting depth charges and everything else. Nobody knew what was out there, but we sure weren't taking any chances that it might be a Japanese sub.

Suddenly he announced to the entire ship, "Secure general quarters. Submarines do not make 90 degree turns at 20 knots." Without elaboration we all knew I must have mistaken a whale for a submarine!

Then dawn broke. It became obvious that there was no Japanese sub. Instead we could see that we had two whales on the port side and one on the starboard side. We were smack dab in the middle of a school of whales. The whales were squirting great blasts of water through their blowholes and it was like we were in the middle of geysers going off in Yellowstone National Park.

After my exciting combat mission against the whales, I was stationed on a destroyer in dry dock on Mare Island Naval Shipyard, about 25 miles north of San Francisco. That's where I was when the first atomic bomb was dropped on Japan. I had never heard of anything called an atomic bomb before and I didn't appreciate the magnitude of what had happened. What I did appreciate was that the war was over.

The night after the war with Japan ended I had liberty, (a short period of time when sailors are allowed free time on shore), and spent it on the streets of San Francisco. It was quite a party. In fact, it was madness. There was no room to walk on the sidewalks or the streets because of the crush of people. You just sort of got pushed along. Everybody was singing or shouting, waving their arms or their shirts or I don't know what all. I've never seen anything like it since that night. We were all so tired of war.

About two weeks later, I was on my way to Shanghai and had just been assigned to the *USS Kenmore*. We were headed out to replace the veteran sailors and to bring back ships for decommissioning. As we were sailing away, I looked back at the panorama of the Golden Gate. As we looked toward the Fort Baker hills, we saw a huge sign — as big as the Hollywood sign in Los Angeles — that read, "WELCOME HOME BOYS, JOB WELL DONE!" I laughed to myself, relieved that the war was over and that I never had to see combat.

Americans weren't the only ones tired of war. I found that out when the Navy shipped me out to Shanghai in the autumn of 1945. Even though the war was over, my service was not. I wasn't discharged until August 1946.

In Shanghai we tied up at the Huangpu docks, which were full of huge bomb holes. All the lights had been blown away, so you had to watch where you were going or you could end up in the drink. There we worked with Japanese minelayers, still manned by Japanese seamen. Through interpreters, we told them that we had their charts where they had laid all the mines in the Yangtze River. We told them to sweep for every one of those mines — they brought them to the surface and we would destroy them with rifles. It was unbelievable how fast the Japanese

The most action I saw during the war was when
I mistook a whale for an enemy submarine.

seamen found those mines. They wanted to go home so badly.
They had enough of war too.

Before we got to China, we stopped in Okinawa. It was full of
military carnage. I saw an old four-stack destroyer of ours from
World War I that was split in half — part of it settled in the shal-
low water, and the rest had rolled 90 degrees and had water
washing in and out of two of the four stacks. And we found hundreds of deserted Japanese suicide boats. These were boats that
carried bombs and had a detonator in their prow, designed to
ram into Allied ships and destroy both of them. But at the end of
the war, no one wanted to kill themselves for a losing cause. So
they just ran the boats up on the beach, jumped out of them and

ran off into the jungle. Some of them hid in the jungle for years. You can't blame them, can you? I guess they hadn't read Tojo's diaries, which were made public years later. He wanted every last Japanese to stay and fight even after the atom bombs were dropped, until everyone in Japan was dead. What a madman.

When the Vietnam War came along, I was too old to worry about enlisting. I never really understood why we got involved in Vietnam. I remember listening to JFK and thinking, "What is he talking about?" Were we after oil? Were we trying to defeat the whole communist bloc just by going after one small country? I never did understand why we should fight and die in Saigon instead of Moscow or Beijing, if we were trying to defeat Communism.

At the same time I was no supporter of those crazy draft dodgers and war protestors who were all over our streets during that time. Since I was in Northern California, I lived right in the heart of those nuts and I saw what they were really like. They claimed to be peaceful, but those peaceful marches often created violent chaos.

I had a personal experience with this nonsense during the height of the unrest in the 60s. I had a contract at UC Berkeley to demolish concrete and haul it away to the dump. The first day we dug out a small tree with a backhoe and set it on the ground. As soon as we did, a girl pulled up in her Volkswagen and picked up the tree, stuck it through the window and drove off with it. Just stealing in broad daylight! Later that day, we were loading concrete that we'd just broken on the sidewalk. We had 10 dump trucks lined up on University Avenue and an army of these protesting animals climbed up on the trucks, jumping up and down on the cabs and yelling obscenities. I had no idea what they were protesting or why they picked on us. One of the guys driving a dump truck came up to me and said, "I'm going home. You can take this job and shove it."

I went up to the guy in control of the contract and told him I was pulling all my men and equipment off the job and that I was going to exercise the clause in the contract about riots and insurrections. So we packed up and left. Later on I found out that those nuts were protesting about building student apartments on the land, although I'm not sure why they thought that was so bad. But since they disagreed, they went up and down Shattuck and University Avenues breaking store windows. And then they had the nerve to say they were for peace. I call violently demonstrating for peace a contradiction in terms. Because you're mad about one war, you start another war. Is this a sensible way to handle conflict?

War breeds madmen and the bigger the war, the more madmen you have. During World War II we had Tojo, Hitler and Mussolini — enough evil to last a thousand years and yet we had them all at once.

That evil takes a long time to go away. In 2000 my wife Lucy and I visited Israel. We went to the Holocaust Museum. The reality of war, the reality of the evil that war unleashes, hits you right in your gut in a place like that. It's hard to take, but at least it's real, they don't pretend it never happened. When we visited Germany in the late 90s, I found that the modern Germans don't want to talk about Nazis or World War II. "That's a sickness my ancestors had," seems to be their view. I think it would be healthier if they learned from what their ancestors did. I understand that they must have had a hard time coming to grips with their history, but so do we all. There isn't a country on Earth who hasn't plundered or raped or even murdered, somewhere in their past. The Germans aren't alone in this, or the Japanese, or the Russians, or the Chinese, or the Cubans, or the Arabs, or the Americans. What we all are is human, capable of stupidity and violence that can escalate into war.

It just never seems to stop, does it? One war might end, but there are two or three more going on to take its place. Back in the late 1980s, I wrote a letter that I was going to send to someone in government, although I never did. I called it "A Cure for Insanity" and it was about how we could control future violent clashes if we would work to put together a world peacekeeping force — a world military unit that no one individual nation could challenge.

At the time it seemed like the world was coming apart again. The Russians had just shot down a South Korean airliner with a US Congressman on board. They claimed it was in Russian air space. (Air space — that whole term is stupid.) The situation was tense. I'd lived through one world war and I didn't want to go through another. I didn't want my kids to go through what I did.

So I wrote a letter, or maybe it was an article, proposing that all the nations of the world maintain a naval, land and air force that would be many times superior to any individual nation's ability to amass a combative force against it. This superpower would not be meddling in internal affairs of any country, but instead would be dedicated to wielding total authority over any military threat. It would serve as an international police force aimed at maintaining world peace.

This concept is not new. It has been idealistically rattled around in novels and movie scripts for years, but has never been seriously considered in the real world because it threatens the sovereignty of any individual nation. But it seems to me that in any individual nation the sovereignty of a smaller subdivision is already handed over to a larger subdivision such as a city to a county, a county to a state, a state to the nation. All this does is extend that — the nation to an alliance of nations. Then we would have a world power which was totally controlled from the bottom up.

The mix of personnel in this military force would have to be in a constant state of flux to prevent the danger of one group taking over. The leaders in control would be fed from the individual subscribing nations. No individual nation could be represented beyond its direct population representation as one measure, and its economic and scientific ability as another measure, such as we have in various parliamentary houses of representation throughout the world.

In the letter I used specific examples from the conflicts in the world at that time — the Falklands War and the Soviet clash with Afghanistan were two — to show how this could work. I talked about the huge complexities of setting up such a force and how we could do it — although, like this book, there were holes where I didn't know how we could cross all the Ts and dot all the Is.

My letter was about 16 pages long. People who read it seemed impressed, but convinced me that no one in power would read it. I didn't send it. Now I wish I had. Maybe no one would have read it and it would have ended up in the crank file. But maybe someone would have seen some value in it. I don't know, and it is one of my regrets that I never sent that letter.

The United Nations today is making strides in the direction of world peace that I had envisioned, but it hardly has an invincible military force. I still believe that we have to face the fact that at this point in time, for our own survival, we must create one universal power without peer and without allegiance to any political survival group other than the whole of mankind. We cannot afford war any more.

It doesn't take much of an examination of the universe to realize that if the world blew itself up tomorrow, it would not make one iota of difference in the overall expanse of the universe. No one on Earth even flinches when there's a supernova explosion that destroys an entire solar system out in space, and all we are talking about is blowing up one tiny planet. We must not be so naïve as to think we are the center of the universe when we're on the verge of being vaporized by the creation of our own mistakes. If we cannot control ourselves, no one is going to come to our rescue.

Chapter Sixteen

What Is Justice?

Maybe there is no such thing as justice. It's a truism that life isn't fair. So why do we keep trying to make it so?

Nearly everyone in the United States would agree that we have a problem with crime. Kids as young as 12 have access to automatic weapons. Drug use is epidemic. Gang violence is rampant in urban areas. Many people have taken to putting bars on the windows of their homes. Small businesses get used to being robbed regularly.

Our response has been to make more stringent laws and build more prisons. In fact, we are taking funds away from more publicly beneficial programs and instead are expanding funding for prison construction in the US. Something is wrong here.

Of course there have to be laws. There must be penalties when people break the law. On the other hand, we have to make sure the laws are just. And we have to find a way so people don't keep on breaking the laws.

Currently our criminal justice and prison systems are failing. Prisons are just garages for people who have to be fed. They drain our resources and add nothing in return. When the criminals have served their terms, do they come out of prison with a trade? Have they learned to be a carpenter, a plumber, a bookkeeper or a computer programmer? It doesn't do much good to say, "I make license plates." There isn't a job out there for license plates. It doesn't even do any good to say, "I can work in a laundromat," because even though there are jobs in laundromats there aren't enough of them to keep all the released prisoners busy. So guess what? They're released without hope, so they go out and break the law again. This becomes their profession. This is just stupid. "What do you do?" "I'm a professional criminal. And you?"

I think we should ask how these people got in the mess they're in. Did they just make one big mistake? Or do they have a pattern of making mistakes? Repeat criminals should be treated differently from those who have made one mistake. We need to show compassion for them and show them a way to do better. At the same time we cannot allow people to disrupt society. Compassion is not coddling. The three strikes law has merit. Let's pass more laws aimed at progressive punishment for career criminals. While accenting skills to the potentially trainable, business should be willing to supervise retraining. The prison system contribution is the room and board.

If a 13 year old kid gets his hands on an automatic weapon, we need to take the weapon away from him, but putting him in jail with murderers and rapists is just barbaric. It would be a rare 13 year old who could be rehabilitated in that environment. It's much more likely he'll just get worse.

As an aside, I'm for less government interference, but I favor some gun control. It's ridiculous to claim that the right to bear arms includes automatic weapons. That's about the same as saying the Second Amendment says we have the right to own individual nuclear missiles. Our founders didn't envision that at all. When the Constitution was written, the times were different. People needed their own guns for food and protection. The guns themselves were different. You had to ram a ball down the barrel after pouring the powder in. It took a couple of minutes to get the gun ready to shoot. And that was for a single shot. Now we have guns that can shoot 10 rounds a second. The Second Amendment can be updated or repealed by the same process as prohibition was repealed. At the very least it needs serious updating from time to time.

But we'd have to have gun control that actually works. If you make it too hard to own guns then only bad people will have them, buying them on the black market. It's the same way with drugs. Making drugs against the law doesn't stop the drug problem. It just drives it underground and makes it impossible to institute programs that help drug abusers kick their habits.

I've never taken drugs, but both my wife Lucy and I were four-pack-a-day smokers for over 20 years. It's not as if we didn't know it was bad for us. We knew. I understand that it's not easy to kick an addiction. Good thing cigarettes are not against the law — although why aren't they? There's enough evidence to prove that they are harmful. There's enough evidence to prove that alcohol is harmful too, but look how criminalizing that turned out. Prohibition did nothing to stop drunkenness. All it did was drive it underground and create a huge market of criminal customers that allowed the Mafia to grow into a force that drained our justice system. Why is drug abuse treated so differently? Drug addicts need help, not prison sentences.

I'm not soft on crime, though. Repeat criminals should be treated in a harsher way than someone who made one big bad mistake. They should be housed in different facilities, so they don't infect the ones who have a chance at rehabilitation. Criminals should be given psychiatric evaluations and let the psychiatrists determine who goes to which facility.

At the bottom of the criminal chain, where you find the chronic offenders, the child abusers, murderers, arsonists, rapists, serial killers — those people should not be coddled. I don't believe they can be rehabilitated. Can you rehabilitate a Ted Bundy, a Jeffrey Dahmer, a Charles Manson? They are lost souls and we should simply give up on people like that. It's not like the world is short of people — why keep these mistakes around? It costs several million dollars to incarcerate just one serial killer. Maybe we can use them for psychiatric studies to discover how not to produce someone like them, but they're not of any other use. They contribute nothing. All they do is swell the prison population.

This is why I am in favor of capital punishment, a question that has been hotly debated for decades. There are well-intentioned people on both sides of the issue.

I have personal experience to back up my opinion. One of my cousins was murdered by a serial killer. She was bludgeoned to death. Her father found the body. My cousin Gordon and I helped to clean up her apartment after the police were done with it. Wall to wall blood, graphite fingerprint dusting and gore. This was over 30 years ago and yet today if I close my eyes I can see that scene. Only a monster could do something like that.

The murderer was on the run for nearly 20 years before he surrendered due to a national TV exposé for another murder in another state. He was never tried for my cousin's murder and died in Attica New York State Prison.

About 10 years after her murder I was called for jury duty. It was a murder trial. On a questionnaire they asked the potential jurors if we could render a fair verdict. I had to say no. I said it out loud in front of the whole jury pool, the judge, the defendant, his counsel and the district attorneys. They took me into chambers and asked me to explain why I couldn't give a fair verdict. I told them the story of my cousin and the impact her murder had on our family. How one family member became an alcoholic because of their inability to deal with the enormous grief and anger. How Gordon and I washed down the walls of her apartment. How none of us were the same again. The judge asked both the defense attorneys and the prosecutors if they wanted to keep me on the jury; they both said no. They couldn't get rid of me fast enough.

So yes, I think that chronically violent murderers should pay for their crimes with their lives. What does society gain by keeping them alive? But I know that capital punishment is not something to be taken lightly. We must always keep in mind that our judicial system needs to truly work. There have been too many cases in the last 10 years, since the advent of DNA technology, where we've discovered that some people who we thought were guilty were actually not. Hopefully that same DNA technology that has shown us our mistakes will help to prevent us from making more.

We will still make some, of course. That's what the appeals process is for. But if the appeals process is as broken as the rest of the system, how will we get justice?

I think we just have to keep trying, whether justice exists or not. Two of my daughters are in law enforcement. Both of them say they chose their profession because they wanted to serve others. Even after years in this field, where burnout and cynicism are common and exposure to the lowlife of society is a daily occurrence, they both continue to believe in the value of what they do. Although justice isn't always achieved, mostly it is. And that's what makes it worth it.

Chapter Seventeen

Why Do We Work?

Work is not a dirty word. Why do so many people talk about work like it's a necessary evil? It may be necessary, but it's not evil. Work is what makes life interesting. I bet Adam and Eve in the Garden of Eden were pretty bored with nothing to do all day except sunbathe and eat low-hanging fruit.

Anyone who grew up during the Depression knows that work is a privilege. I remember the look of defeat and despair on the faces of people without jobs, including my own father. When I was a kid, I didn't know we were poor — I hadn't connected money to work yet. What I did see was how helpless my father was without his job. It was like he had no idea who he was without it: if he wasn't a teacher, or even a fruit picker, who was he?

And even though in those days most women didn't work outside the home, that didn't mean they didn't work. My mother worked so hard even I noticed it, young as I was. She was always cooking or cleaning or sewing or gardening or helping out the neighbors. Plus she did work outside the home when it was necessary; she was a bookkeeper, hiring herself out to a dry yard or a plumbing supply house to do their bookkeeping. Then after my parents divorced, she had to find full-time work to support my sister and me.

During the Depression the adults talked about two things all the time: jobs and money. Nobody took either for granted. If it cost money, we saved it. We saved string, we saved tinfoil, and most of all we saved food. It was a sin to waste anything. Somebody worked hard for that food. People worked for food directly too. I remember people going door to door, asking if they could mow your lawn or weed your garden in exchange for a meal.

President FDR's New Deal programs were based on work, not on handouts. Some of his programs failed; some of them were even stupid. But it was important he did something rather than nothing. He got people moving again, working again — even if they made little money. The Work Projects Administration (WPA), the National Recovery Act (NRA), the Civilian Conservation Core (CCC) — the people in those programs worked damn hard for a modest paycheck. The money was necessary, but what was really important was the work. Work and self-esteem go together.

Today my kids tell me that I think about money too much. But I don't think we see money in the same way. To them, money is the things they can buy. To me, money is the work we put into getting it. They don't understand what it's like to live without money and with little hope of getting any. They're spoiled in the sense that life is a lot easier now than it was when I was a kid. But we're the ones who spoiled them. I certainly don't want my kids or grandkids to go through a Depression just so they will learn the value of work, but there's no doubt it's a good way to learn it. This isn't to say they don't have a good work ethic because they all do. But they don't know what it's like to go without work because it has always been available and abundant.

About six months after my parents' divorce, when I was almost 15, my mother told me, "You eat as much food as your sister and I put together. So you have to get a job and pay half the food bill."

It's true; my appetite was nearly legendary in my family. One of the family stories that gets told every family reunion is the cantaloupe story. I was visiting my Aunt Laura and Uncle Eddie, and my cousins Allan and Roy. It was right in the middle of the Depression and money and food were tight. One night there was going to be a meteor shower, so we boys decided we'd sleep outside on the lawn to watch it. We had a great time and the next morning we woke up hungry, as we always did. Aunt Laura said she'd take us to buy some fruit for breakfast. So we piled into her black 1937 Ford and went down to the produce market. There

My partners in cantaloupe crime, Allan and Roy.

Aunt Laura decided to buy a whole crate of cantaloupes, because they were a good deal — 50¢ for 24 cantaloupes.

When we got back, Aunt Laura went in the house leaving us boys to unload the crate of cantaloupes. I don't remember whose idea it was, but somehow we decided to have a cantaloupe eating contest. We sat down on the lawn and ate through the whole crate. Allan was the loser; he only ate four. I came in second; I ate seven. Roy was the winner because he ate the rest — thirteen cantaloupes. I don't know why he didn't die. I don't know why I didn't throw up, but I managed not to. When Aunt Laura came outside she was appalled. "What are your father and I going to have for breakfast?" she demanded. Nobody ever let us forget that day, not because we made ourselves sick, but because we had wasted food.

So because of my big appetite, my mother decided I had to carry my share of the family load. She took me to get my social security card, which was issued in 1942 right before I turned 15. I still carry that social security card in my wallet today. It's a little beat up by now, but it's got a right to be — it's 69 years old.

The first job I got was delivering the Oakland Shopping News. Soon after that I worked in a grocery store for four hours every night after high school. I bagged groceries and hauled boxes for 65¢ an hour. Next I got a job in a machine shop for 85¢ per hour, and finally after that I hit what I thought was the mother lode — I worked on the ovens at Continental Baking Company, making Wonder Bread. I made $1.34 an hour and felt pretty good about it. Not only because of my great wage, but because I loved Wonder Bread. It cost 12¢ a loaf and tasted — well, wonderful. We ate a lot of it while I was working there.

I've been a hard worker all my life. And although sometimes the work has been difficult, frustrating and even painful at times, I like working. Although money is important to me, work isn't just about money.

Single with a good job. *Summer, 1951.*

After I was discharged from the Navy, I went to junior college for 18 months on my GI bill. Then I got a job through the California Department of Employment working for Henry J. Kaiser Motors. I worked there for eight years, making my way up the ladder to West Coast Assistant Manager for the Wholesale Parts Division. I was responsible for the dealer structure in 10 western states, so I had some authority. But I didn't think I made enough money, especially after I got married and we thought about having a family. My job paid $434 a month, which in 1956 was decent money, but not great. I thought I could do better on my own, if I worked hard enough.

So I took a gamble and quit my safe job at Kaiser and went into the excavating business, getting my Excavating Contractor's License and a General Engineering License. Because of my work at Kaiser I was very knowledgeable about the products. One of those products, a trenching machine mounted on a jeep, was the backbone of my business. After three years with the jeep we bought our first backhoe. That's when things really took off. My wife Lucy quit her job as a social worker and ran the office. We both worked our butts off and we made our business one of the most successful small backhoe excavating firms in Northern California. We had our fingers in many of the major construction projects of the 1960s and 1970s. I am proud of what we accomplished, proud of the money we made and especially proud of how hard we worked.

Financially, the hard work in our business paid off even more than when my cousin Gordon offered us a share in a family partnership in 1960. As I mentioned before, this enabled us to buy real estate and capitalize on the building boom in California. After 10 years we built a warehouse. Eighteen years after that, we bought an old manufacturing plant, both of which we still own and lease today. It has been my experience that hard work leads to success, and success leads to more success. There's no magic about it.

I tried to teach my daughters about the importance of work and the value of money. I don't know how successful I was. None

In my first business after I quit my good job. Working in excavation eventually earned me the nickname "Dirty Don the Ditch Digger."
April, 1956.

of them have done as well financially as we have, but they are all successfully employed and able to support themselves and their families. They're all hard workers.

I remember when they got to be teenagers Lucy and I wanted them to have a separate phone line put in the house just for them. It's true that they got most of the phone calls at that time. We thought it would be a good way to teach them about money, so we said we'd pay for the basic phone bill but they had to pay any overages they ran up.

The very first month there was a 35¢ charge for a misdial to Crockett, a town about five miles up the road. My oldest daughter didn't think she should have to pay it since it was a misdial. But it was on her phone so I said she did have to pay it. Someone had to pay for that misdial after all. We argued about it and she was in tears she was so mad at me. My wife Lucy wanted to give in and just pay it. "It's only 35¢," she said. "Why are we arguing about 35¢?"

But we weren't arguing about 35¢. We were arguing over a contract we had made. I stuck to my guns and our daughter eventually took the 35¢ out of her babysitting money. Did this teach her anything about money? I think so. And I think it taught our second daughter, who was watching the whole thing. She is now a penny-pincher, sort of like her parents. She budgets her money carefully.

I try to pay as I go and always have. I have to admit though, that on major purchases in business I've had to finance equipment that justifies its existence by generating a profit beyond the burden of the loan (principle and interest). I worked hard for my money, but I don't feel like I have to flaunt it all over the place. I live in a tract house among thousands of other people, even though I could afford a more upscale one. I've been here 34 years and have no plans to move. Money gives me the ability to live well, but it also gives me the chance to give back to the community and country where I've lived and the places that have given me the opportunities I've had. Warren Buffett, one of the richest men in America, still lives in a house in the middle of Kansas. Not exactly a glittery palace. He's still a frugal man. He worked for what he has too.

When I collect my monthly rents I always carry two coins with me. One is a Sacajawea dollar, the other is a penny minted in 1845. Someone always complains that I raise the rent every year. So I pull out the coins and tell them their money is always changing value. Things don't cost the same as they used to. I used to buy off-road diesel for 14¢ a gallon. In the last few years it's gotten as high as $5 a gallon for highway diesel. You have to pay attention to money or it dribbles away pretty damn fast.

Work is what lasts. The government can help people who need it, but it doesn't owe you anything. It can't do it all. Those programs during the Depression got us working again; they didn't give away something for nothing. We all have to work and we all live in a community, so our work has to benefit each other. Work is how we define ourselves. Work is how you pay for the great fact of being alive.

Chapter Eighteen

Does Gender Matter?

We spend a lot of time thinking and talking about sex and the differences between men and women. Nowadays it's "in" to think that those differences don't matter. I don't agree — they do matter. Why is it politically incorrect to say that there are some things that men do better than women and other things that women do better than men? It sounds like plain common sense to me.

Less than two pounds of the body weight of a male is devoted to reproduction. But a major portion of a woman's body is devoted to reproduction and the care and custody of an infant. That's a difference that's hard to ignore. All females carry the the very "temple of life." Without females mobile life cannot exist.

If human beings stay out of it, there will naturally be close to a 50-50 split between the number of boy and girl babies born. The universe tends toward balance. Men are built one way to do certain kinds of tasks and women are built in another way, to do other certain kinds of tasks. Why mess with what works?

Why are women smaller than men? Why do women's hips jut out unless it's so they can park a baby there? When one of our daughters went through the police academy, she had to prove that she could physically do what a man could do. She had to go through the same steeple chase. She had to put her body over a six-foot wall by pulling herself up a rope to the top. I didn't think she'd be able to do it, not because she wasn't determined or physically tough, but simply because she was so much smaller and lighter.

Well, I was wrong. She did make it through, but it wasn't because she proved her body was as strong as a man's. It was because of her guts, determination and drive. Sometimes I think women have more staying power than men. They can carry an infant around for hours and not turn a hair. I can't carry one on my hip for more than five minutes.

But I'm still not sold on women doing jobs they're not physically able to do. Why should a woman be expected to take on more danger than a man, just because she's a woman? That's what it means when a job requires strength or speed that is past a woman's capability. She'd be in more danger than a man would. Maybe I feel so strongly about this because I have three daughters and I hate the thought of them being exposed to danger. I'm a father, after all. I want to protect my girls. Even though I've gotten used to the idea that I can't protect them, I don't have to like it.

We acknowledge this truth in sports. In the Olympics we have different competitions for men and women. Women swimmers don't compete against men swimmers. The women's soccer teams don't play the men's soccer teams. Because if they did, guess what would happen? All the men would win.

Well, maybe. Remember the Billie Jean King verses Bobby Riggs tennis playoff in 1973? Riggs challenged King to a playoff, boasting that she was no match for him by mere virtue of his manhood. She ended up beating Riggs in three straight sets. I guess there are always exceptions to any rule.

People are probably thinking by now that I'm one of those male chauvinist types. But this is not true. I am absolutely in favor of the equality between men and women. Even in sports and physically demanding jobs, I'm in favor of equal opportunity. I think that girls should be able to play Little League softball just like boys. I just don't think they should play against the boys. I think that women should be able to be cops or firefighters or heavy equipment operators — if they can handle the work and they don't put themselves or their coworkers in danger. And of course I'm for women being business executives, doctors, lawyers, scientists, artists, astronauts, or anything else they can dream up. I'm glad all those stupid gender stereotypes that used to keep women "barefoot and pregnant" or in "pink collar jobs" are gone, or going.

During my lifetime there has been a radical change in how our society sees gender roles and I've been cheering the women on the whole way. I've always known that you can't lump all women together and claim that they all want the same things or feel the same way. They are separate individuals, just as men are. Even if I didn't know this before, I certainly would have learned it as the father of three daughters and the husband of one of the most unique and capable individuals I have ever met, my wife Lucy.

Perhaps I learned to value and respect women as individuals because of my mother. She worked outside the home at a time when most women didn't. She was a divorced woman at a time when that was supposed to be a shocking thing. It never occurred to me to think there was anything "wrong" about her. I always respected her and was proud of her.

So when the Women's Liberation Movement came along in the late 60s and 70s, it didn't make much of an impact on me or my wife. My wife Lucy was college educated and was always a working woman. She ran our business office: she was the finance department, the payroll department, the purchasing department, the marketing department and the receptionist. There is no way I would have succeeded without her. When our children started coming along, the first in 1960, she continued running the office as well as raising the children and running the home. Things I wouldn't have been able to do in a million years.

The Women's Liberation Movement did have an impact on my daughters, though, especially in the social attitude toward education. Up until then it was generally felt that women didn't need a college degree. Many people thought that the women who did go to college just went to catch an "MRS" degree — to marry a well-educated husband who could support them in style. After all, you don't need a degree to get married and keep house. This wasn't necessarily true, of course. My wife Lucy had a college education and was working as a social worker before I even met her. Like my mother, you could say she was ahead of her time.

Well, the attitude is different now. Women now get an education for themselves, just like Lucy did. All my daughters, who came of age in the late 1970s and 1980s, went to college as a matter of course. They didn't go to catch a husband; they went to help them figure out what job they wanted to train for. All three of them today have good jobs and they make a difference in their communities. How can you not be happy about that?

So I approve of many of the changes made in the last 30 years, especially for women. But I can't say I approve of all the changes the so-called sexual revolution brought into our society. Some people would call me a prude, but the overt sexuality in movies and TV, or in books and music — that crap that's in your face all the time — it just leaves me cold. It's bad enough that many teenagers don't think anything of having dozens of sexual partners by the time they settle down. But nowadays there are little kids of eight who know more about the mechanics of sex than I did when I was eighteen. We've made it so that sex isn't special any more.

But I don't recommend that people stay ignorant about sex, either. I was as innocent as a choir boy for a long time, but it wasn't because I was a prude. It had a lot more to do with fear.

When I went into the Navy at 18, one of the first things they did with us recruits in boot camp was show us a movie about sexually transmitted diseases (STDs), which at that time was called venereal disease. The image that really stuck with me and that I can see today if I close my eyes, was a South Sea Islander who had contracted elephantiasis because of "loose living," or so the movie claimed. His testicles were so huge he had to trundle them around in a wheelbarrow. I nearly threw up while watching that movie.

A couple days after we'd seen the STD film, a bunch of us went down to Tijuana on liberty. Dozens of little kids were swarming around hawking their sisters. They would come right up to us and say, "Hey, want to have sex with my sister? Only $5." I wasn't even tempted. All I could think about were those enormous testicles. It took me a long time to get over it.

It's even more important today to be educated on sex — real education, not the titillation and pornography you get through the media. Back when I was young, STDs made you sick. But now we have AIDS. These days stupid sex can kill you. I don't know anyone who doesn't know someone who has died from that awful disease. One of my oncologists died of it, two years after he successfully treated me for leukemia. He was somewhere in his 40s, I believe.

And some people think that there should be no sex education in schools! What can they be thinking? Teenagers aren't stupid, unless they are allowed to remain ignorant. It's not just disease, either. It's girls getting pregnant while they are still children themselves and boys who refuse to be any kind of father. When my wife Lucy was a social worker, she worked with girls as young as 13 who got pregnant, or with young women of 20 who had six children already with another on the way. This is insane. It affects everyone: the school system, the welfare system, the criminal justice system. It's insane because it's preventable. And it's ludicrous to think that putting condoms in the schools' vending machines will promote promiscuity, when those kids can go home and watch TV programs showing naked people having sex. I think pornography promotes promiscuity. Education promotes responsibility.

The other thing that sexual license promotes is divorce, which is an epidemic in the US. If you jump from bed to bed before marriage, why shouldn't you jump from spouse to spouse? What happened to "let's work it out"? As a society, marriage doesn't seem to mean what it used to mean. Now the thinking seems to be, "If things get tough, run." My wife and I were married for 54 years, which is something I am extremely proud of. We had our share of problems and tough times, but we worked it out. We didn't run.

I know about divorce because my family is riddled with it. My parents, grandparents and several aunts, uncles and cousins have divorced, some of them several times each. I've rarely seen anyone improve their situation by getting one. All they do is jump into the same problem with a different face. It's usually three marriages before they finally decide they're not going to win this stupid game. Why not stick with the first one? Why go through the trauma? And especially why put the children through the trauma?

Now obviously there are legitimate reasons for people to divorce; I would be negligent not to acknowledge that. What I'm talking about, though, are those that enter into marriage with a throwaway mentality. And unfortunately there seems to be more and more people that do.

My parents split up when I was 14. When I was 15 I had to go to work and help my mother put food on the table because she had to bring up my sister and me without much help from my father. He paid the court assigned child support of $35 per month per child, plus $1 per month alimony. He never paid a dime more. And even in the 1940s that was not enough to live on.

After their divorce my father ranted to me about how my mother turned me against him. That was not true. She never once said anything bad about him to me, but he was still complaining about her on his deathbed. And what really made me angry with him was that he left us and broke up our family. He didn't care enough about me or my sister to try to work it out with my mother. Of course, I don't know what their problems were; maybe they were bad enough to warrant a divorce. But that's how I felt.

Yes, men and women are different and sometimes those differences come into conflict. But we are all human beings and our differences are not as important as our similarities. Deep down we all want the same thing: love, respect and people who keep their word.

Chapter Nineteen

What If...?

This book has asked a lot of questions and proposed a few answers. It seems evident to me that we better come up with a lot more answers if we want to survive. That means I must believe it is possible there are answers to be found. At least some answers, at any rate.

But what if I'm wrong? What if there are no answers, because the universe is governed by totally random forces over which we have no control? Maybe we are simply victims of the winds of change, or "hostages to fortune" as Francis Bacon put it. Maybe we have no input into what happens to us. Maybe the answers don't matter.

It's hard to prove this by peering blindly into the future. But when you look into the past, the argument for the random nature of the universe becomes viable. We can examine that awesome word "if." Just a couple of examples will do.

Scientists believe that 65 million years ago an asteroid crashed into Earth in the area of what is now the Yucatán Peninsula in the Gulf of Mexico. They say this event changed Earth's climate so severely that it led to the extinction of the dinosaurs. They had been here for 140 million years and then disappeared.

What if that asteroid had missed Earth and hit Mercury instead? Or Venus, or the moon, or just sailed into a black hole somewhere? Thousands of asteroids miss us every year. Some of them come pretty close. Other planets have been vaporized by asteroids. Many scientists believe that it's just a matter of time until another asteroid hits us again.

So if that asteroid 65 million years ago had missed us, would life as we know it have evolved at all? If we did evolve, how would we have escaped being a dinosaur's dinner? Okay, maybe that example is too far away and too long ago. Let's take another few examples closer to home.

On December 6, 1941, the US Pacific Carrier Fleet was heading home to Pearl Harbor from maneuvers out at sea. They were due to arrive in the early hours of December 7th. However, that evening a storm blew up and held them up about 400 miles away from Pearl Harbor. If that storm had not come along at that time, the whole American Pacific fleet would have been reduced to impotence by the Japanese attack at eight o'clock the next morning. What if the storm had struck a few miles away from where it did? What if the Japanese attack came at noon instead of 8 AM? What if the Japanese had won the war?

Another example from World War II: in 1945 the *USS Indianapolis* delivered the only two atom bombs in the world to the island air base where the Enola Gay B-29 was based. The Enola Gay delivered the bombs to Hiroshima and Nagasaki. But that's not the "what if" I want to point out.

On the return trip from the island air base, the *Indianapolis*, unescorted and under the blackout conditions common in wartime, was sunk by a Japanese submarine. What if she had been sunk on the way to the island instead? What would have been the effect on the war? How much longer would it have gone on? And what if we had a couple of undetonated atomic bombs at the bottom of the sea?

The *Indianapolis* "what if" has a personal meaning for me. When I was serving in China in late 1945 to 1946, I was assigned to a sub chaser. I was 18 years old and my skipper, who was nearly as green as I was, showed me and the rest of the crew a classified blueprint. It was stamped "For Your Eyes Only." This blueprint was for the invasion of Tokyo Bay. It showed the positioning for each ship's assigned location, with only our ship identified on the perimeter. We could tell by the sizes of the various ships on the blueprint where the capital ships were to be positioned. The skipper had been ordered to destroy these plans, since the atom bomb had made them unnecessary. It was supposed to be very secret, but as I say, he was green. He saw to it that it was incinerated after the viewing by the crew.

A slight change of circumstances and I would have seen combat.
Instead – thankfully – a whale was the highlight of my Navy career.

If we had not bombed Japan, it is likely the war would still have been going on. Tojo was not going to give up. The invasion of Japan was to be on the order of Normandy. The estimate I heard was that they were going to put one million men on the beach. I don't know if that is true or not — rumors are not very reliable. That certainly would have put my ship in a combat position.

And it probably wouldn't just have been Tokyo. Without the crushing blow of Hiroshima and Nagasaki, we might have had to take on every major city in a Normandy-style invasion. The population of Japan at that time was around 80 million. The carnage would have been unbelievable, both for them and for us. Would I have survived? I don't know and I'm glad I didn't have to find out.

"What ifs" are not usually as big as asteroids or atom bombs. Often big things hinge on small, unrelated events. You probably have "what if" examples in your own life. I know I certainly do. For instance, if it weren't for a dead battery in my sister's car I

My wife Lucy and me on our honeymoon in Lake Tahoe. Happenstance brought us together. *August, 1955.*

never would have met my wife Lucy. My sister was on her way to visit a friend, but when she got in her car it wouldn't start. She asked me to take her there and bribed me by saying that her friend's roommate was kind of cute. I reluctantly agreed. When we arrived I met the cute roommate — that was Lucy. By chance a dead battery led me to my wife of 54 years. If we could find that dead battery, I'd have it bronzed.

So to the question I posed at the beginning of this chapter — do we have any control over our lives, really? In spite of the power of the word "if," I believe the answer is yes, we do. Because no matter what seemingly random thing life throws at us, we are still are in charge of our actions and reactions. Why did the battery in my sister's car die when it did? I don't know, and it doesn't really matter. What matters is that when it did, I gave my sister a ride. It is our choices, not our circumstances, which define us.

Chapter Twenty

Humpty Dumpty Earth?

Is the earth itself cracking because of human activities? Is it as fragile as an egg? We are consuming every last drop of oil, which will be gone forever in just a few centuries. Other raw materials such as copper, iron, manganese and others are not renewable resources. The consumption of all these natural resources is leaving cavernous pockets as human activities accelerate. Why don't we realize this? Are we too ignorant, or do we think we are so clever we'll be able to figure a way out? Or are we just blasé and uncaring about the generations coming after us?

We are approaching extinction. We rely on experts to guide or influence our behavior because we individually are ill-equipped to function, or even survive, on our own. If we don't find experts to guide us, an individual's thinking is limited to his or her own life span, focused solely on the unique hand they were dealt. Can't we assemble enough rational thinking experts to realize that we are the shepherds of our own existence?

The wars raging on our planet, each inspired by political or religious loyalty to win at any cost, are taking us faster along the road to extinction. We must wake up to the realization that patriotism or religious ideals are limited to human-created boundary lines and inspired by eloquent, but often empty, words. For us to swear allegiance to a piece of colored linen on a pole is ridiculous. While nations are competing to be "King of the Mountain" and religions are preaching, "We're the only one," the earth is increasingly vulnerable to being vaporized a few billion years before natural evolution takes over.

The best brains of our experts are creating ever more insidious Weapons of Mass Destruction (WMD). Is this really the best use of human creativity? The only possible argument supporting continued development of WMDs is the slowing effect on overall population totals. That's hardly the best answer. Wouldn't it be better to educate the public to plan on manageable sized families?

We must ask these questions, over and over, again and again. We must ask our leaders and especially we must ask ourselves. I know that when we answer one question, two more will pop up in its place. There is no end to questions. But even if we don't have the answers yet, we must keep asking.

Here's the only real answer, to any of the hundreds of huge questions facing us: become aware. Wake up, in other words. Find solutions to these problems. We have made some modest gains in this area, but unfortunately people don't want to become aware because they may have to blame themselves instead of somebody else. We all want to point the finger and say, "It's too big a problem. I'm just one little person who can't do anything." We need to admit that this is not true. If you take a clothes hanger and hang all the problems of the world on it, it would break. And what would you have left? Just the hook: ONE BIG QUESTION MARK!

Now it is your turn to help solve these problems. Take off one problem at a time from the clothes hanger and solve it *before* it breaks. If we all did something, no matter how small, we could solve our problems. If we all educated ourselves by asking questions and demanding answers, perhaps our descendants will have a chance to appreciate the beauty of life on this incredible planet.

For in the end, if we don't ask questions, we really are nothing more than chickens who can't learn algebra.

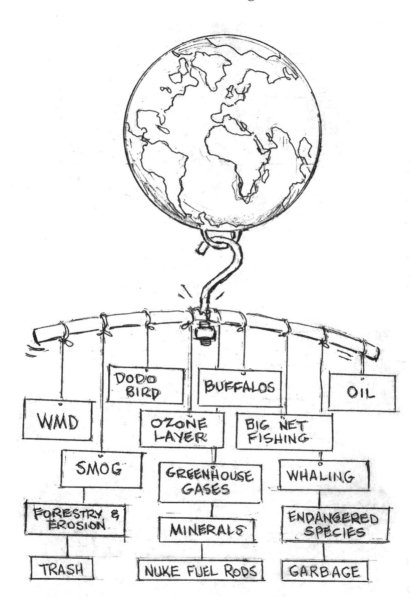